W9-DCJ-971

THE ENGLISH PARISH CHURCH

OTHER BOOKS BY RUSSELL CHAMBERLIN

The Count of Virtue: Giangaleazzo Visconti, Duke of Milan
Everyday Life in Renaissance Times
Life in Medieval France
Marguerite of Navarre
Cesare Borgia
The Bad Popes
Fall of the House of Borgia
The Sack of Rome
Rome (Time-Life Great Cities of the World)
Florence in the Time of the Medici
The World of the Italian Renaissance
Preserving the Past
Loot: the Heritage of Plunder
The Awakening Giant: Britian in the Industrial Revolution
Life in Wartime Britain
Everyday Life in the 19th Century
Great English Houses
English Market Towns
The National Trust: the English Country Town
The Idea of England
The English Cathedral

The English Parish Church

Russell Chamberlin

with photographs by Simon McBride

NA
5461
.C44
1993
sc ob

Hodder & Stoughton

LONDON   SYDNEY   AUCKLAND

THE UNITED LIBRARY

British Library Cataloguing in Publication Data
Chamberlin, E.R.
English Parish Church
I. Title
942

ISBN 0-340-58650-8

Copyright © Russell Chamberlin 1993
Colour photographs copyright © Simon McBride 1993
First published in Great Britain 1993

All rights reserved. No part of this publication may be reproduced or transmitted in any form or
by any means, electronic or mechanical, including photocopying, recording, or any information
storage and retrieval system, without either prior permission in writing from the publisher or a
licence permitting restricted copying.
In the United Kingdom such licences are issued by the copyright Licensing Agency, 90
Tottenham Court Road, London W1P 9HE. The right of Russell Chamberlin to be identified as
the author of this work has been asserted by him in accordance with the Copyright, Designs and
Patents Act 1988

A ·DELIAN·BOWER· Book
with acknowledgements to Webb and Bower (Publishers) Ltd
Conceived and edited by Delian Bower
18 Devonshire Place Exeter EX4 6JA England

Published by Hodder and Stoughton, a division of Hodder and Stoughton Ltd,
Mill Road, Dunton Green, Sevenoaks, Kent TN13 2YA
Editorial Office: 47 Bedford Square, London WC1B 3DP

Picture research by Anne-Marie Ehrlich
Designed and typeset by John Youé, Honiton
Printed in Great Britain by Butler & Tanner Ltd
Frome and London

ACKNOWLEDGEMENTS

The Publishers would like to thank the following for
supplying illustrations.

COLOUR

All colour photographs by Simon McBride

BLACK AND WHITE

G H Bunting: 154

E T Archive: 137, 138, 141 (left and right),
142, 151, 153, 164 (above and below

Clive Hicks: 171

Courtauld Institute of Art (Conway Library): 89

Hulton-Deutch Collection Limited: 163

A F Kersting: 39,71 (centre), 72, 73, (left and right), 77, 84, 85, 88,
95, 102, 105, 106, 107, 113, 114, 115, 121, 124, 125, 172, 173

Mansell Collection: 162

Norfolk County Council: 74, 75

RCHM England: 58, 62, 66, 67, 70, 71 (above and below), 91

Shropshshire Records and Research Unit: 96

Edwin Smith: 17, 18, 21, 23, 25, 28, 29 (above and below), 37, 38,
44, 45 (above and below), 46, 48, 50, 51, 53, 54, 55, 56, 57, 80, 81,
82, 86, 89, 90, 128, 167

Parson Woodforde Society: 155, 157 (above and below)

Contents

Colour Illustrations

INTRODUCTION

W e take them for granted, these extraordinary structures which strive to give physical form to an invisible truth.

Even today, in many a village and small town the church is the largest building, the only one where the community can meet as one. And in all too many an urban or urbanized locality it is the only building of any distinction. The twentieth century, for all its technological skills, has lost the art of town-building, flooding green spaces with mass-produced structures which belong to no particular region and rarely seem intended much to outlast the lives of their builders. The parish church provides an identity in such amorphous localities to remind the residents that they have a past.

Unlike the lordly cathedral whose design is the result of continental-wide movements extending over centuries, the local church is literally born of its community, its creation the work of local men, completed within a single lifetime so that it faithfully reflects its period. Unlike cathedrals whose materials may be drawn from many miles away, the materials of churches are drawn from the earth around them: glass-like flint in East Anglia, golden stone in the Cotswolds, sombre granite in Cornwall. Their towers are like banners proclaiming their local allegiance: the gaunt elegance of Suffolk's stepped structures, the cheerful exuberance of Somerset's or the solid dignity of Yorkshire's.

Despite the decline in church attendance, the dilution and confusion of religious belief, the local church is far more truly the social heart of the community than the consciously designed 'community centres' of the post war years. On entering a church one can immediately assess the prosperity of the community, reflected in the physical condition of the building. Somewhere there will be a children's corner, an area in the vast structure made humane with bright posters and small chairs, flowers and perhaps a piece of carpeting where the local children will absorb the idea that there have been others before them. (The children of Pevensey have written a history of their church which is on sale inside). Near the main door will be a table covered with pamphlets: pleas for famine relief in

Africa; reports on missions in exotic places; the church roster, and invariably, financial appeals. Unlike their continental counterparts the state contributes little or nothing to their physical upkeep and the fact that they survive, that somehow vast sums are raised in small communities to repair the roof, restore the organ, renew stonework, is testimony to the loyalty upon which the church can still rely.

On the table, too, will be the church history, written by a member of the community with varying degrees of expertise, a pamphlet costing a few pence and quite literally priceless for it will be obtainable nowhere else and contains information related only to the locality. Far more than the sacred buildings of its related religions, the synagogue and the mosque, far more in indeed than its counterparts in most continental countries, the English church is the repository of the corporate memory embodied in the crammed memorials of those who have gone before. Anyone in quest of the history of a village, or even a town, automatically gravitates to the church before the library, if there is one. An excellent example of the church as communal memory is Southwater in Sussex. The village is almost entirely a nineteenth century industrial creation arising out of the brickyards and the twentieth century's contribution is a 'village centre' in the anonymous 1960's eggbox architecture. The little church of Holy Innocents is also nineteenth century with no particular features – except an extraordinary sequence of stained glass windows made in the 1980's. Modern stained glass is only too often pretentious abstract or mawkish 'Gentle Jesus' confections. Holy Innocents' windows are superb 'light pictures' illustrating the daily life of the community. Whatever there is of Southwater's identity is vested in its little church. Finally, at the heart of this structure is the enigmatic figure of the priest or parson, changing outwardly from century to century but discharging an unchanging role. A tyrannical figure in the seventeenth century, the object of ferocious satire in the eighteenth, of sentimentilization in the nineteenth, and of polite tolerance in the twentieth, he is the direct descendant of the oldest authoritative figure in the human community, the tribal shaman, coming into his own at the traumatic moments of birth and marriage and death.

The present book tries to draw these elements together and create a 'biography' of this mysterious institution. Strictly speaking, not all the churches which are discussed are 'parish churches' for, as explained in the Appendix, the term has an exact legal meaning which often excludes some of the most interesting churches. However, the term 'parish' has been retained in its wider sense for although it has been downgraded so that 'parochial' is now almost synonymous with 'trivial', the word embodies that powerful sense of local patriotism which was the cornerstone of English local government until the nineteenth century reforms and is one of the themes of this book.

CHAPTER I

THE EARLY CENTURIES

Tucked away in the tangle of country lanes a few miles south of the sprawling town of Reading in Berkshire, is one of the most poignant relics of Roman Britain — the buried city of Silchester. Poignant, because unlike most of our ancient monuments which have been dissected, analysed, interpreted, and 'conserved' until every element of mystery has fled, Silchester looks today much as it would have done some 15 centuries ago, after nature had reclaimed what the Romans had abandoned. The great protecting wall survives around most of the site, but in places huge roots of trees have penetrated into its vitals. As the Saxon poet who on encountering such a ruin in the sixth century, vividly lamented:

'The grasp of the earth, stout grip of the ground
Holds its mighty builders who have perished and gone.'

Within the walls there is little to see now, for although from time to time archaeological digs have traced out the plan of the city, the earth has been shovelled back, burying and protecting it. In 1891 a small, undistinguished building was excavated near the forum. Its existence was recorded, speculations made as to its purpose, and then it was again returned to the 'stout grip of the ground'. In 1961, however, it was again unearthed and detailed investigations with modern techniques disclosed that the little building (it measures some 42 feet by 33 feet — less than the ground area of many a modern suburban house) was a church. This is, therefore, the oldest surviving building erected as a church in Britain.

It is not, however, by any means the only Christian related building which survives from Roman Britain. On the banks of a little stream called Darent in Kent, lie the remains of one of the three great Roman villas of Britain, Lullingstone. Although the existence of the villa has been known since at least the eighteenth century, it was not until 1949 that systematic excavations disclosed its elaborate nature. Begun about AD200, it shows continuous development over at least 300 years, becoming ever more luxurious. As with all long-standing buildings, successive occupants adapted it for their own uses. Around 360, the then occupant evidently became a Christian and turned an upper room of the villa into a handsome little chapel. On the walls appeared what must be, the first example in Britain, of those wall paintings which were to become so popular in churches during the Middle Ages. Here, a group of people appear in ceremonial robes, holding up their hands in the gesture of prayer customary in the early centuries of the Church. Nearby is the unequivocal indication that this room was dedicated to the Christian god and no other, for here dramatically plain, is the sacred chi-rho symbol on a roundel.

At about the same time that the Lullingstone occupant was having his home committed to the care of Christ, another wealthy man in Dorset was paying to have an elaborate mosaic made on the floor of his villa. The significance of two of the roundels have caused much earnest debate among historians of Christianity. In one, the chi-rho symbol again appears, again unequivocally indicating the room's Christian significance. Superimposed on this symbol is the face of a clean-shaven man, dressed in Roman fashion, and flanked by pome-granates — the recognized symbol of eternal life. All indications are that this must be a formal representation of Christ, certainly the earliest in the country. Nearby, however, in an equally prominent position, is a mosaic showing Bellerophon slaying the Chimera. Was the owner of this villa hedging his bets, proclaiming his allegiance to the new religion while prudently retaining contact with the old? Or was he simply a cultured man who saw no reason why an ancient myth should not be placed alongside a modern truth? Either interpretation is possible.

These three survivals — the unadorned little hut in Berkshire, and the rich men's ornamentations in Kent and Dorset — are all dated around 350. That year is about midway between the martyrdom of St Alban in 304 — the first clear indication that Christianity had arrived in Britain — and the beginning of the retreat of the Roman legions in 410. To anyone in the following century, that year of 350 must have seemed the very peak and apogee of Christianity in Britain, for with the retreat of the legions it would have seemed that Christianity too was in full and fatal retreat. The new religion doubtless survived in remote pockets, taking shapes that would have startled sophisticated southerners. But in distant Rome it must have seemed that night had returned to the western isles. It was then, some time about the year 604, that Pope Gregory was supposed to have been enchanted by the two little Saxon slaves and, murmuring his epigram — *Non Angli sed angeli* — sent his missionary Augustine to save the souls of such beautiful people.

But what Gregory probably did not realize was that on an island even further west than Albion, an island that for the Romans must have seemed on the very edge of mythology, Christianity had not only survived, but had flourished. The Celtic Church in Ireland had somewhat changed its form from that recognized by the Roman Church: it had a different date for Easter and dedicated its churches to the founding monk rather than to a patron saint. Above all, it was inward looking and monastic in impulse, unlike the cosmopolitan Roman Church. But it was as urgently desirous of saving souls. About the time that Augustine and his band of 40 missionaries were cautiously working their way through south-east England, anonymous Irish missionaries were moving down from the north and west. Given the usual way of settling religious differences, one might have expected a violent encounter. But astonishingly, the vital question as to which form of religion would rule England — the Celtic or the Roman — was settled peacefully at the Synod of Whitby in 664, when Rome emerged triumphant.

The Celtic Church, though, left two impressions on the nascent Church in England: the one physical, enduring down to our time; the other administrative which shaped the local, or parish church, until the coming of the Normans. The physical related to the shape of the ground plan. Augustine had brought from Rome the plan with which he was naturally most familiar — the great Roman law court or basilica, with its solemn double row of columns and the rounded apse where sat the chief magistrate and his entourage. This apse was invariably at the western end of the basilica and was naturally the place of honour chosen for the altar. When the altar, for unknown reasons, was moved to the east, the priest, following that conservative instinct which is the leitmotif of religion, continued to face West — thus standing with his back to the congregation. The Celtic plan for a church was far simpler: a rectangular cell, without aisles and with a smaller rectangular cell attached to its east end. This became the chancel and, with a few exceptions, it is the square Celtic chancel, not the semicircular Roman apse, which has been transmitted down the centuries.

The second enduring impression left by the Irish was the pattern of their missionary activities. It is one of the ironies of history that it is Augustine and his glamorous Romans who have the credit for converting England, whereas much of the work was done by the Irish. Their activities were based on a mother church or minister whence missionaries would venture out into the wild. In these early years, this grandly named 'mother church' would have been a simple building — perhaps nothing more than a chapel in some great man's house. But whatever the limitations of its architectural nature or dimensions, the role of this mother church was awe-inspiring. Here, and here alone, could a person receive that baptism which would put him or her among the ranks of the saved. Here, and here alone, were kept the keys of Heaven and Hell. From this mother church emerged the missionaries, carrying their intangible message and their tangible altar further and further afield. As the distance increased from the mother church, so there would be an arrangement for the setting up of the altar in some easily recognizable spot. There might be half a dozen or more of such 'daughters' ministered by the 'mother'. In the still featureless countryside where towns were rarities and villages little more than a handful of scattered huts, there was a need to set up some form of identification. The natural indication for a rallying point would be the Cross — first in the form of a simple wooden structure, then as time passed, evolving into an elaborate stone, carved with the intricate designs so much admired by the Saxons. They survive still in many a churchyard. One of the finest examples is that at Eyam in Derbyshire, where this enigmatic monument, richly carved with human figures, looms above the plain tombstones of later centuries.

On news of the coming of the missionary, the local populace would gather round this symbol of the faith to hear the message of the Gospel and receive the sacrament from the hands of the priest. But it was still necessary to go back to the mother church for baptism. In these first years of Christianity, baptism was by full immersion. The baptismal font was correspondingly massive, and quite apart from reasons of sentiment, it made practical sense for the people to go to the font rather than bring the font to the people. But it was also the means whereby the mother controlled the apron strings, as it were. Three times a year the faithful were urged — commanded — to return to the mother church and there make their vows and pay their offerings. These three ceremonial pilgrimages, at Christmas, Easter, and Whitsun, became social as well as religious events — a welcome break in a harsh, monotonous life.

Inevitably there developed over the decades the desire on the part of a daughter church to have an identity in her own right. The driving spirit behind the establishment of a permanent local church would usually be the thegn, forerunner to the Norman baron. He had the organizing ability, the wealth, the power to donate land and to draw on a labour pool. In return, he would have the immense prestige of having, in effect, his own private chapel. Out of this process grew the English system of 'squire and parson' — the one giving, the other receiving: a relationship which would have endless repercussions on the country's social, religious and cultural life.

Physically, the local church might be an actual part of the thegn's great hall or might simply be in the locality. Over a millennium later one can still see the effect of this symbiosis, sometimes with distinctly odd results. At Deene Park in Northamptonshire, seat of the Brudenells (the most notorious member of the family being Lord Cardigan of the Light Brigade), the church is entirely in the grounds of the park. At Arundel in Sussex, seat of the dukes of Norfolk, there is an even odder manifestation. The dukes are Roman Catholic, the local parish Anglican. There are therefore two entrances to the parish church, the one approached from the castle and leading directly into the Roman Catholic section of the church, the other approached from the town and leading into the Anglican nave.

The reason for the siting of the 'estate' church is self-evident: the convenience of the patron and the availability of land. But the majority of our ancient churches are independently sited. The reason for any particular site being chosen is by no means obvious and is frequently downright mysterious. Siting does not necessarily conform to any of the topographical or economic criteria which dictate the siting of all other buildings. The church may be at very considerable distance from the village over which it is supposed to be presiding. At Salle in Norfolk the immense church seems to be stranded among fields a good two miles from the village. In some cases it can be shown that the village moved away from the church, attracted perhaps by some new industrial development or the re-alignment of an important road. But others provide no such easy answer: at Knowlton in Dorset there are the ruins of a twelfth century church in the middle of an earthwork and no nearby village at all. A clue lies in those surrounding earthworks. Again and again one finds that an apparently eccentrically sited church is standing in or near man-made earthen mounds. At West Wycombe in Buckinghamshire the church stands, dramatically, inside an immense earthwork which itself crowns a hill. At Pyrford in Surrey, Moreton in Dorset, and Taplow in Buckinghamshire the church stands on a large circular mound. Added to this topographical clue is the etymological one. The Latin races derive the name for their sacred building — their *eglise* or *chiesa* — from the Greek *ecclesia*, meaning a regularly convoked assembly. The Teutonic nations take their *kirche* or their church from the Celtic *ciric* or 'holy ground'. Thus the Latin peoples regarded their church as being essentially a meeting place, whereas the northern peoples regarded it primarily as a building placed on an already sanctified spot. It was not indeed until the tenth century that the idea of *ciric* was transferred from the ground to the building. Put at its simplest, the church was placed in the churchyard and not the other way round with the churchyard developing around the church. The Christian building crowned and dedicated to Christ an already sacred spot.

Here, in concrete and permanent form is enshrined a basic example of how the Church absorbed and conquered. Pope Gregory had specifically instructed his great missionary, Augustine, to adapt, not destroy. The idols, indeed, were to be thrown out for they flouted the unbreakable law of the Second Commandment, but the place where the idols had been set up had been already sanctified by human love and longing:

> 'Let these become temples of the true God so the people will have no need to change their place of concourse'.

Augustine was encouraged to go even further. Aware of that human desire for continuity, for tradition, the Pope urged the missionary to countenance even the sacrifice of animals:

> 'Where of old they were wont to sacrifice oxen to demons in this matter also there should be some substitution of solemnity: on the day of the saint to whom the church is dedicated, or the feast of the martyr whose holy bones have been set there, let them slay their beasts no longer as a sacrifice to the devil but in honour of him whom they worship.'

Here, as early as the seventh century, is the genesis of the rumbustious 'church ales' of the Middle Ages. One can see the villagers on a feast day, drifting towards some long-hallowed spot — a circle of standing stones perhaps, or a distinctively shaped hill dedicated to some local hero — and there, in that familiar setting, go through a familiar ceremony, though one with a different dedication. Looking back over the turbulent, bloody history of Christianity, particularly in the sixteenth century, one wonders what shape it might have taken had other pope's followed Gregory's wise tolerance.

The communal sacrifice to a local, transformed, deity has vanished into history, but in the very stone of many of our churches is preserved evidence of the great transformation from pagan to Christian. On a corbel in the church of St Mary and St David in Kilpeck, Hereford & Worcester, is an extraordinary figure which, if executed

St Boniface, Bunbury, Cheshire.
Norman elements survive, but this is a characteristically
Perpendicular Cheshire building.

St Andrew, Greensted, Essex. The oldest timber building in Europe.

*The Abbey Church of St Mary the Virgin, Sherborne, Dorset.
Mostly rebuilt after 1420.*

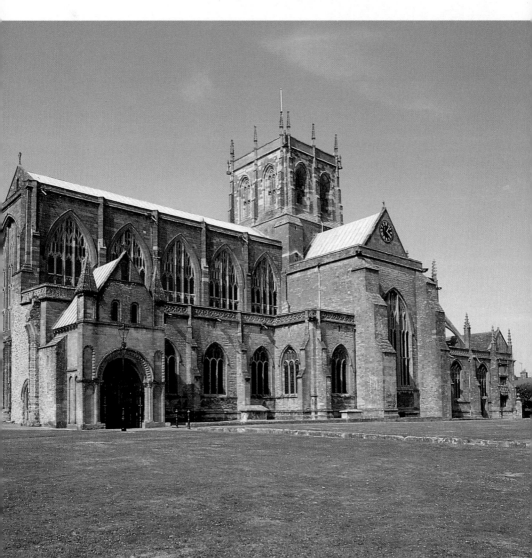

Crypt of St Wystan, Repton, Derbyshire.
The church virtually grew around the crypt for it was originally
designed as a mausoleum in the seventh century.
It was re-discovered by accident in the eighteenth century.

Pagan beliefs died hard, as evidenced by the extraordinary figure of the sheelagh-na-gig *on the church of* St Mary and St David, Kilpeck, Hereford and Worcester.

today, would have the perpetrator charged with obscenity and blasphemy. Known as a *sheela-na-gig*, it depicts a female figure holding apart the lips of her genitals in a gesture which combines mockery with invitation. When one considers the monuments which have fallen to the fury of the iconoclasts it is truly extraordinary that 18 of these representations of the Earth Goddess should have survived in churches around the country. Even more common is the Green Man, a male human face peering through a dense screen of leaves, frequently with branches actually growing out of his mouth. In the more carefully executed examples of this mask, such as one on a misericord in Holy Trinity, Coventry in Warwickshire, the leaves can easily be identified as those of the oak tree — the tree that was sacred to the Druids.

The gathering place marked by a Cross and already known to the locals would have sufficed for the first wave of missionary activities. A semipermanent shelter for the altar and officiating priest would doubtless have come into being and it would be only practical common sense to erect some form of shelter for the embryonic congregation. It may be as early as this period that there sprang up the distinction between what was to be the two sections of a church: the sacred area or chancel where the priest officiated, and the nave — the secular area accommodating the people. But soon these rough and ready shelters would be deemed unworthy and the people themselves would plan and erect a structure intended to be permanent though using the traditional building material of timber.

In the first two or three centuries of the Christian era orientation seems to have been unimportant. In the very heart of Christianity, in

Rome itself, 40 out of 50 of the early churches have their sanctuary at the west, continuing to follow the tradition of the basilica. In Britain, however, certainly from the early Saxon period onwards, orientation became standard practice, and how this was achieved has produced another of the myths relating to the early Church. A history of Freemasonry, published in 1859, firmly encapsulates this myth. The night before the orientation ceremony, which took place on the feast day of the saint to whom the church was to be dedicated:

'The patrons, ecclesiastics and masons assembled and spent the night in devotional exercises. One, being placed to watch the rising sun gave notice when his rays appeared above the horizon. When fully in view, the master mason sent out a man with a rod which he ranged between the site of the altar and the sun, and thus fixed the line of orientation'.

This description does, perhaps, have the advantage of explaining why few churches face the true east, for the orientation would naturally change with the changing season. But one need only consider how, in Britain's variable climate, it would be extremely difficult to predict that sunrise would be visible on a given day, to realise that orientation must have taken place on a fairly hit or miss basis. With orientation completed and the dedication made, work would start on the actual building.

The Venerable Bede, writing in the early eighth century, referred admiringly to a certain Benedict Biscop who built the monastery at Jarrow, Tyne & Wear, about the year 670: 'He was the first man to introduce into England builders of stone edifices and makers of glass windows'. It may well have been true for the important monastery at Jarrow and for a handful of other outstanding buildings, but for the vast majority of these early churches, building materials would consist of some variant of wattle and daub. How flimsy such a structure could be is illustrated by a legend of St Cuthbert, first recorded as late as the twelfth century and quoted by Salzman in his monumental work on medieval building. A village youth climbed on the buildings:

'There was a little church dedicated to the honour of St Cuthbert constructed of unhewn branches [ie branches in their natural state] And because the wooden walls by reason of their great age had rotted inside, whenever he placed his foot to climb up, the weak osier gave way and in many places he broke and pierced the wall. Suddenly his feet and the branches under him flew out and he fell down, breaking nearly all the joints in his bones'.

The wattle which formed the framework was a form of basketwork. A row of solid stakes, or trunks, was set in the ground, and the spaces in between filled with flexible material — hazel rods, reeds, osiers — whatever was available locally. Clay, mud, or in some advanced cases mortar, was then forced into the interstices. Hair, straw or clay was then worked into the plastic material to make it cling properly, the whole being smoothed over and given a coat of whitewash. Used in interiors, or when otherwise protected from the weather, this method of construction proved remarkably durable, lasting for centuries. But used on an unprotected exterior, as in most cases, its life would be necessarily brief. The next stage would therefore be the timber church proper.

We have become so accustomed to building in brick and concrete and stone that we tend to regard wooden buildings as being somewhat second-rate, temporary structures. Until the renewed use of brick in the fourteenth century, however, and for perhaps two centuries afterwards, the majority of buildings in England were either completely of timber or at least timber-framed. In a heavily wooded land, profusely producing one of one of the best of all building timbers, oak, would naturally turn to this universal and cheap material. As far as the Anglo-Saxons were concerned, it was so much *the* constructional material that their word for 'building' was quite simply, *timbrian*. Great ship builders, they turned their carpentry skills to churches. How durable was their work is well illustrated by the survival of Greensted Church in Essex, archaeologically established as being the world's oldest wooden building, beating even the veterans of Norway by a generation. Built about the year 1013 as a resting place for the remains of the martyred King Edmund, it has been, like all ancient buildings, successively adapted and changed over the centuries, and now incorporates everything from Norman flint to Victorian brickwork. But the south wall of the nave has remained completely unchanged: massive trunks of oak, roughly adzed stand on a horizontal timber sill. It has been calculated that the now blackened tree trunks were probably growing at the time of Christ and legend has it that the covers of the church's Bible and prayerbook are made from the tree against which Edmund was martyred. The legend had a substantial boost in 1848 when the ancient tree fell and an eleventh century arrowhead, was found embedded in the trunk.

It is perhaps fitting that the first clear indication of the new way of building should be linked with Alfred, one of the few monarchs in history to deserve his soubriquet of 'the Great'. In pursuit of a vow

The Norman imprint: the tower was added to this Saxon church of St Andrew, South Lopham, Norfolk, in the first quarter of the twelfth century.

at Athelney, in Somerset, this truly universal man

> 'made a church small indeed in area but contrived in a new manner of building. For four pine trees embedded in the ground carried the whole edifice.'

Did these pine trees denote that crossing (the junction between chancel, nave, and transepts) which was to be a standard feature of cruciform churches and thereby make a radical departure from the simple oblong cell of the Celts? If so, this gives Alfred yet another outstanding 'first'.

The survival of Greensted church can be regarded as being due to an oversight. Although the Saxons were accustomed to timber and perfectly happy to use it for their own residences, the house of God required more permanence, timber must yield to the nobility of stone. As the land grew more prosperous and settled, Saxon masons began to take over the building of churches from their carpenter colleagues, this was at least four centuries before the arrival of the Normans.

At about 5.30pm on the evening of 14 October 1066 the leader of a small army or skirmishing force, numbering about 5,000, was killed in battle and his men overwhelmed. The small band of victors then proceeded to take over the country. They were promptly joined by others of their compatriots from the Continent, scenting loot. But even a year after the Battle of Hastings it is doubtful if the Normans, their allies and auxiliaries numbered altogether more than about 30,000. The kingdom they were taking over had a population of between half a million and a million.

The Norman Conquest of England is one of the profound mysteries of history. Never before, or since, has so limited a military action — one whose conclusion was in doubt almost up to the end — had so immense a cultural and psychological effect. Even now, 1,000 years afterwards, the English bear the scars of their first and only defeat and conquest as a nation: dropping their usual cavalier attitude to other people's languages they attempt to pronounce French place names in the French manner, thereby earning the mockery of the French people.

The trauma of the Conquest has served to influence the popular view of pre-Conquest England. It is as though a thick red line had been drawn through history at the year 1066. All before that line is viewed as being somehow barbaric, as though there were little difference between the land that William of Normandy conquered and the land conquered by Julius Caesar. Culturally Saxon England was, with one exception, at least the equal, and in the sphere of

The sense of mystery in a Saxon church:
St Laurence, Bradford-on-Avon. A view across the nave looking
into the north porch.

imagination, probably the superior of Normandy. The exception was in architecture, and even here it was a difference of degree, not of kind. Saxon and Norman architecture sprang from the same source, that harking back to Classical Rome and now known as 'Romanesque'. Where the two peoples did differ in this matter was in the vast energy of the Normans and their prediliction for the massive and the grandiloquent. In the generation following the Conquest they threw themselves into an astonishing building programme which saw the creation of a multitude of castles to hold down the populace as well as a programme which saw the birth of most of our great cathedrals, abbeys, and major churches. Unlike the Saxons, who preferred to tinker and adapt — a characteristic they bequeathed to their English descendants — the Normans preferred the clean sweep and were prepared, if need be, to demolish one of their own buildings in order to create a more splendid one. The major buildings of Saxon England disappeared under that furiously creative onslaught. So it is to the humble parish church — in particular the church in a village or small, unimportant town, overlooked or temporarily bypassed by the Normans — that one must seek the true Saxon heritage.

There are identifiable remains of at least 250 Saxon churches in England but only a handful of these are as their masons left them. Outstanding among them is the noble little church of St Laurence in Bradford-on-Avon, Wiltshire, which paradoxically owed its survival to neglect — and its restoration to a remarkable piece of historical detection. After a grand new parish church was built in the twelfth century this tiny church endured a series of degradations. First it served as a charnel house and then was physically transformed into an ordinary dwelling house complete with chimney, then a school. At one stage it was even used as a shed for a factory. A nineteenth century engraving shows it hidden among surrounding undistinguished buildings, the elegant arcading of its chancel alone indicating its origin. In 1856 a vicar of Bradford, intrigued by the dignified appearance of this 'shed', in particular by the two great flying angels on the nave wall began investigations. In the Bodleian Library he discovered a work by William of Malmesbury which described a small church built by St Aldhelm in Bradford towards the end of the seventh century. Over the next half century the church was carefully restored and is now a perfect example of a small Saxon church.

Despite its small size, the only adjective that can describe St Laurence's is 'noble'. Built of the same honey-coloured stone as the rest of the historic buildings of the town, it combines both the Celtic and the Roman traditions, illustrating emphatically that Saxon architects were perfectly well acquainted with Romanesque styles. The

*The Saxons, when they chose, could build on as monumental a scale
as the Normans, as shown by this view of All Saints,
Brixworth, Northamptonshire.*

ground plan is purely Celtic, consisting as it does of nave and chancel, with very little difference in size between them. The two sections are entirely separated by a massive wall, pierced by a low and narrow doorway. The chancel is, in effect, a hidden area rather reminiscent of a Jewish Holy of Holies. This desire to create a truly sacred, almost hidden place, is a very Celtic characteristic. It is possible, indeed, that in the early days of the Celtic Church the high point of the mass — the consecration of the sacrament — took place behind curtains drawn around the altar. In this little church there is, even today, a feeling of intensity of devotion, and intensity perhaps created by, and certainly heightened by, the lack of light and the narrow space. But if inside all is Celtic mystery, the exterior is all Roman logic and lightness with an elegant arcade visually binding chancel to nave. The inspiration for this must somehow have come direct from northern Italy, passing through who knows how many minds before Saxon masons raised this exquisite little building above the Somerset water meadows.

Escombe church in County Durham, from the same period and of the same style, is an entirely different proposition. Instead of being situated in a delightful riverside town, it is set dourly in a semiderelict industrial area. Its material is not the light-enhancing stone of Somerset but the dark, grim millstone grit of the north. But its association with Rome is even more direct than that of Bradford's church, for here it is not simply a case of transmitted skill, but many of the actual stones come from the Roman camp at Binchester. One of these has been carelessly put in upside down and reads, starkly and significantly LEG VI — the Sixth Legion. Another relic of Rome is a stone, set sideways and forgotten for centuries until, in 1969, a schoolboy noticed that the scratches on it read *Bono Rei Publicae Nato* (to the man born for the good of the state). There have been few changes to the church since it was completed some 1,300 years ago. Sometime just after the Conquest, a fastidious or pedantic priest had a piscina put in the south wall, a porch was added in the twelfth century, and enlarged windows help to lighten the sombre interior a little. And that is about all.

Grandest of all the Saxon survivals is the church at Brixworth, Northamptonshire. Like Escombe, Rome contributed on a lavish if involuntary scale. The brickwork of the arches, which stand out dramatically against the dark ironstone were plundered from some Roman building. It has not, as with Escombe and Bradford, survived unchanged. The aisles which marked its basilican nature have vanished and the belfry and spire were added in the fourteenth century. But enough survives to show that the Saxons could, when they wished, build on a monumental scale.

CHAPTER II

THE MEDIEVAL BUILDERS

In 1817 a Liverpool architect, Thomas Rickman, looking back over the rich confusion of architectural styles that had prevailed in England, made a well meaning attempt to bring order out of the chaos. He announced:

> 'English architecture may be divided into four distinct periods or styles which may be named: first, the Norman style: second the Early English style: third the Decorated style and fourth the Perpendicular style.'

According to his calculations the first three styles each lasted for a century, beginning from 1066, while the final, Perpendicular style, lasted for two centuries — from 1350 to 1550.

It was a useful enough device even though it did beg the question of what happened during the nearly 300 years between the 'end' of Perpendicular and Rickman's own day. (And from our own perspective, of course, it provides no guidance whatsoever during the truly chaotic, eclectic nineteenth and early twentieth centuries). As long as Rickman's classification is recognized as being a very crude rule of thumb, it can be used to create some kind of chart or overview of the immense changes which took place during five centuries: from the England subjected by the Normans, to the England ruled by the Tudors. But it is only a rough approximation. As soon as Rickman made his offering, however, it was adopted as a kind of iron law. A given church had to be Norman, Early English, Perpendicular, Decorated or something called Transitional. The limitations of Rickman's Law are immediately manifest when applied to a building which has existed for centuries. Unlike cathedrals, most churches were built well within a lifetime — but it is a rare church indeed that

The restrained elegance of the Perpendicular style is well illustrated by the delicate traceries of these windows:

(Above) The south aisle window at St Peter and St Paul, Leominster, Hereford & Worcester.

has not experienced endless changes over the succeeding centuries: changes brought about by increased wealth, by new fashion, by fire (always a hazard in a building stuffed with tinder-dry timber), by the erosion of sheer age.

Apart from architectural changes which directly affect the church, are the changes in society itself. Admittedly, social changes took place at a far slower pace throughout the Middle Ages than they do today. Builders in Tudor England were as dependent upon animal and human muscle power as their predecessors five or ten centuries earlier. A Norman mason would have had no difficulty whatsoever in using the equipment of his Tudor successors. The liturgy, the heart of the whole structure, changed in detail, but not with the sudden, literally shocking changes of the late sixteenth century. Money, though circulating far more freely, was not the ultimate measurement of power that it was to become. Nevertheless, gradual though the individual changes were, their cumulated effect was immense. To

(Below) The east window of St Catherine, Ludham, Norfolk.

(Above) The east window of St Mary, Tiltsey, Essex.

assume that the society which created Perpendicular in the mid fourteenth century was the same kind of society which saw its end two centuries later is manifestly absurd. Generations of architectural writers, however, felt themselves obliged to try and thrust their subject into this bed of Procrustes.

Allied to this architectural straight jacket is the common historical habit of assigning neatly clear-cut causes for vast social changes. But though it would be an absurdly mechanistic view of history to say that the Black Death of 1348, with its huge loss of labour force, caused the adoption of the less labour intensive Perpendicular style, it would be a sterile view of history not to recognize that changes in architectural design did indeed reflect changes in the outside world produced by both economics and fashion. Starting from that climacteric date of 1066, one may ask: If there had been no Norman Conquest would there have been so drastic an alteration in architectural styles? The answer must be a qualified 'Yes', for even the insular Saxons would not have been immune from the great tide of innovation that swept across Europe in the early eleventh century.

In recent years, it has become fashionable to cry down the once commonly held view that Christendom expected the world to end with the ending of the first millennium. But there is, in fact, an excellent contemporary witness not only to this belief, but also to the feeling of universal relief that the year 1000 had come and gone without the expected apocalypse — a relief that found architectural expression. The witness is a French monk, Raoul Glaber ('the Bald'), and in his chronicle written about the middle of the eleventh century he recalls:

> 'It seemed as though all the world were throwing off its slumber to clothe itself anew in white churches, and though many were still in good condition, they vied with each other in erecting new buildings, each one more beautiful than the last.'

But though change would undoubtedly have come to England, it would have come without the speed and unprecedented range contributed by the Normans. So widespread is their physical impact on our historic landscape that we have come to take their work for granted. But there can have been no impact like theirs before in history, not even by the Romans whom they so greatly resembled. Within a generation of the Conquest they had altered the appearance of English civilization. Not only were they erecting, or transforming into permanent stone, the immense castles with which they were holding down a highly intelligent, deeply resentful population, but they were also engaged in throwing up dozens of enormous buildings — abbeys, monasteries, palaces, the greater churches — most of which were larger by far than any building ever erected before in the land. In the more important towns, the modest little Saxon church was either demolished outright or altered out of all recognition. New churches sprang up where none had been before. The Normans were perfectly prepared to use Saxon labour: given the scale of their operations and their own relatively limited numbers, they had little choice. Gloucestershire in particular has churches where the lighter, more fanciful mind of the Saxon mason is imposed on, or is side by side with, the Norman (another rich source of confusion to the Rickman Law). What the Saxons thought of all this activity is well summed up by Wulfstan of Worcester. By the year 1080 he was the very last of the pre-Conquest bishops, and looking back over the frenetic activity of the previous fourteen years he shook his head sadly,

'We labour to heap up stones, but we neglect the care of souls. We, poor wretches, destroy the work of our forefathers only to get praise for ourselves.'

Then he displayed that innate Saxon conservatism, that reluctance to accept change, which perhaps made them the inevitable victims of the energetic invaders:

'The happy age of holy men knew not how to build stately churches: under any roof they offered themselves as living temples of God.'

It is instructive to compare that lamentation with his contemporary, Raoul Glaber's, whoop of delight in recording the new age.

There is no mistaking a pure Norman building: the massive pillars like elephants legs bearing massive, rounded arches; the interior dark; the exterior dourly thrusting down on the earth — an excellent badge for the people who created it. Hindsight personalizes this architecture, seeing it as the means whereby the arrogant invader sought to cowe the vanquished. But it was also a result of architectural unsophistication: the only way the Normans knew how to obtain height was by increasing the breadth. And that desire to reach upwards was not matched by technology: the annals of church building are filled with the tale of collapsing towers built about this time. Sometimes it happened a few years after their construction, others survived for centuries though inevitably doomed by the haste of their builders.

In a little over a century after the Norman Conquest, the Normans had begun to disappear. Not through plague or rebellion or even emigration, but to the fate that awaits even the most successful conqueror of a larger society — the ineluctable force of assimilation.

> 'Nowadays, when English and Normans live close together and marry and give in marriage to each other, the nations are so mixed that it can scarcely be decided who is of English birth and who is Norman',

so an anonymous contemporary wrote as early as 1180. Architecture reflects that subtle melding. Gone is the massive, brooding, earth-clutching presence. Gone is the sense of weight. In its place has come what Graham Hutton happily calls 'an air of delicate restraint'. In its place has come what Rickman, with nineteenth century chauvinism calls, Early English. This is the result mostly of technological advance, for in the century since the Conquest there occurred one of the few evolutions in masons' tools: the substitution of the more sensitive chisel for the clumsy axe. Again, we are fortunate in having a contemporary witness to identify time, place and nature of change. The choir of Canterbury cathedral was totally rebuilt in 1174 and the monk, Gervase of Canterbury, specifically drew attention to the delicacy of the work, made possible, he says by use of the chisel instead of the axe. 'In the old capitals (of the pillars) the work was plain: in the new ones exquisite in sculpture'. Gothic, another term of rich confusion, had made its bow.

It was Sir Christopher Wren who gave the new style its misleading name. It had nothing whatsoever to do with the Germanic tribe of the Goths. As far as Wren was concerned it was a drastic and most unfortunate departure from the cool balance of classical architecture. By 'Gothic' he meant, simply 'barbaric'. The style, in fact came not from the North but the East. At the end of the eleventh century, during that great re-awakening of architecture noted by Raoul Glaber, the West began to come into contact with the East through the medium of warfare — the Crusades. In the countries of the 'Saracen' the sciences of classical Greece and Rome had been kept alive. While the Western world expended its energies on theological debate, the Arabs built on their mathematical and scientific heritage, creating a new form of architecture. The Crusaders, in their turn, brought back to their own countries the memory of a sumptuous civilization, a civilization enshrined in stunning architecture where elegance and strength went hand in hand. The key to this new architecture, the

St Mary, Nantwich, Cheshire.
The county's major Decorated church, restored 1854-61.

St John Baptist, Little Missenden, Buckinghamshire.
Saxon in origin, it has fragments of important
fourteenth century wall paintings.

pointed arch, had the simplicity of all great innovations and was so vital to the style that the term 'pointed architecture' was used to describe it until well into the nineteenth century, alongside the now generally accepted term 'Gothic'. Graceful in itself, it was a technological breakthrough in that the stresses from above are directed down into the pillars that support the arch, instead of seeking to thrust them apart as in the round arch of the Normans. The effect of this was twofold: it allowed greater height in the building while substantially reducing the diameter of the supporting pillars. The walls themselves became thinner and stronger as the architects gradually adopted the use of ashlar (large, finely prepared blocks of stone) instead of the massive rubble filled walls of the Normans. The interior of an Early English church, compared with a Norman, is characterized by a soaring elegance, the walls pierced by windows which not only dramatically increased the amount of light, but also prepared the way for another feature — stained glass. The pointed arch made its first appearance in France, the land which had triggered off the Crusades. Specifically, it was the great Abbot Suger who adopted it for the royal abbey of St Denis during its rebuilding in the 1130s. He has left a vivid description of how the towering new arch stood the test of a violent storm — no small vindication when it is considered that mortar requires maturity before it gains its full strength. The style crossed into England shortly after and was tentatively used in Durham cathedral, before emerging fully fledged in the immense new choir at Canterbury.

But if the Normans had begun to disappear as a distinct racial group, the energy they had transfused into the English continued unabated. Between 1150 and 1250 there was an astonishing outburst of church building. Much of this was secular — that is, non-monastic. During the formative years of Christianity in England — throughout the Saxon period and into the Norman — the influence of the monastery had been overwhelming. By 1150 there were at least 500 monasteries in England. Their contribution to the country's cultural and economic life is, quite literally, incalculable. The founders of most new monasteries followed the austere edict of the great Cistercian, St Bernard of Clairvaux, and established their new foundation in remote countryside. There, over the decades and then the centuries, they built up a core of civilization, a reservoir of wealth which nurtured the infant lay communities attached to them. For good or ill, their control over the new churches was absolute. As a matter of course they harvested the tithes and provided parish priests out of their own number. But gradually, as wealth increased in the country and, in particular, as towns began to achieve a sense of identity, so local communities more and more expected to both create and control one of the greatest of all symbols of local pride — the church. They were helped by the formidable king, Edward I, who, alarmed by the manner in which the great religious houses were cornering the wealth of the kingdom, enacted his Statute of Mortmain which strictly controlled endowments and bequests to these great houses.

Edward's statute redirected rather than eliminated the pious offerings of the faithful. It has been calculated that during the twelfth and thirteenth centuries perhaps 50% of the national income was being channelled into the building of churches. A calculation like this is, to say the least, disconcerting to a twentieth century mind with its preoccupation with the vast range of artefacts and services competing for a limited purse. But throughout the Middle Ages, once the personal needs for food, shelter and clothing had been satisfied, and after the local lord had ensconced himself in his stone carapace with whatever luxuries were available, there was little enough to spend money and energy upon, except this gateway to eternal life. In no region is the result of this prodigal expenditure better displayed than in East Anglia, specifically Norfolk, where it is difficult to get out of sight of a church tower looming somewhere out of the flat landscape. In Norwich, by the end of the thirteenth century, there were 25 churches for a population of some 8,000; London had 100 for its population of 40,000 people; in tiny Rutland there were 50 churches – averaging one for every 250 souls. And they were increasing not only in number but in size and grandeur. In many a village a church was erected which could probably accommodate the entire local population several times over. In the early nineteenth century that pugnacious polemecist, William Cobbett, observing the common phenomenon of an immense church in a tiny village, used it to ram home his favourite argument that the population of England had actually declined between the Reformation and his own day.

About the middle of the thirteenth century appeared Rickman's third category — the oddly named Decorated. This was partly the result of an increasingly elaborate liturgy, partly the following of an apparently immutable law whereby ornament progresses from the severe to the sumptuous and back again. Within the church itself there appeared a plethora of structures devoted to specialist purposes: side altars, oratories, chantries, all competing for space which necessitated enlargement of the church. But a change came over the actual form of the church itself: an explosion of design, of crockets and traceries and carvings of every kind. For the layman, the change is most evident in the windows. Over the century they evolved from the elegant, simple 'lancet' of Early English (a tall, plain, rectangular slot usually arranged in groups of three or five), to an extraordinarily elaborate decoration which seems to defy the intractable nature of the material of which it is made and emerge as a kind of web or net. Known as tracery, this transforming of a window opening into a work of art has its own regional variations. Within those variations are yet more sub-classifications: geometric, plate, rectilinear, curvilinear, according to the dominant shape and testifying to the exuberance of the architecture. Then at its very apogee, this style came to an abrupt end, an end coinciding with the awesome tragedy of the Black Death of 1348.

Medieval statistics are notoriously inexact: at times posterity has some justification in the suspicion that medieval Europe shared the same numeration as some primitive tribes, 'one, two, three, many'. The exact proportion of the population who died of the Plague will never be known with any real degree of accuracy. It has been calculated as ranging from one third to one half of the population and even this imprecision is further extended by the fact that it would vary widely from place to place: some localities would suffer nearly 100% mortality while others would escape with an insignificant fraction. Certain classes were more vulnerable than others: the rudimentary medical profession; clergy; the poor who were unable to move from a crowded and infected locality. But whatever the proportion of the dead, there can be no doubting the immense disruption of society that followed. The most obvious was the sudden shortage of labour. This, coinciding with the drastic economic hiatus, simply brought most nonessential activities to a halt. All over the country work stopped on churches. Temporary roofs protected half-finished buildings for thirty years and more and if money and labour were totally lacking in the locality to provide even that protection, the building simply disintegrated. For a generation, the stunned country strove to come to terms with the disaster. The plague returned twice, not on such a scale as the 1348 visitation, but greater than ever known before or since, and it was not until around 1370 that something resembling normality returned. It returned to an entirely changed society. Feudalism was dead. The serfs, upon whose backs it had been placed, were not there any more. Their once despised labour was now seen for what it was, the very dynamic of society and they determined to get the market value for it. It was not achieved without violence, of which the Peasants' Revolt is the most famous. But it was achieved. For the first time, this vast anonymous stratum of society was in receipt of disposable income. Money, instead of being concentrated in the pockets of a relatively few enormously wealthy landowners, was circulating freely — and most of it was passing through the pockets of small traders in the towns.

At about the same time landowners, faced with a depleted and expensive work force turned to the less labour intensive industry of sheeprearing. They discovered that they were sitting on a gold mine. These two elements, the free flow of money and the sudden vast wealth being made out of wool, created the economic wherewithal for the resumption of church building. When the building started again it was in an entirely new form — Rickman's Perpendicular. This, unlike the earlier forms, which, despite the names, Norman, Saxon and Early English were international in form, was a truly English style unlike any other in Europe. It survived for two centuries and encompassed about half of the 10,000 or so churches now recognized as being of historical importance.

Of all the descriptions of Perpendicular, perhaps Olive Cook most memorably and most succinctly sums it up: 'Instead of wild variety, comes uniformity. Instead of mystery, comes clarity'. Decorated is the last, rich flowering of the Middle Ages, the last attempt to allegorize, the last attempt to embody the intangible in wood and glass and stone. Perpendicular is cerebral, a move away towards intellectualism to demonstrate, by using order and logic. The windows of a Perpendicular church provides the clearest expression of that desire — literally the clearest — for in a church like St Edmund's in Southwold, Suffolk, the stonework becomes virtually a framework for the gleaming expanse of clear glass, and the geometric repetition of the window traceries emphasizes the filigree effect. Inside a Perpendicular church, the desire to create unity out of diversity results in the pillars soaring up and becoming the fan vault, perhaps the greatest expression of all Perpendicular features. This is limited to the greater churches such as St Andrew's in Cullompton, Devon, for strong vaulting was far too expensive for the ordinary village church. As compensatory development was the great timber ceiling — less expensive to erect, but giving scope to the skills of the woodcarver. The churches of East Anglia excel in their timber ceilings from the angels of St Wendreda in March, Cambridgeshire, to the portrait and gargoyle faces of St Mary's in Stamford, Lincolnshire. But this exuberance of a timber ceiling is national, not regional. From Devon to Durham it is as though one great creative wave had swept the land and its passing marked one more great change in English society.

The age of most of our parish churches range from 1 million to 500 million years old, for that is the age range of the stone out of which most are built. Until the Industrial Revolution introduced roads and good transport, the vast majority of buildings were created from local materials. In certain areas, such as along the eastern and southern coasts of England it might have been cheaper to bring in stone from

*The church's desire to create unity out of diversity during the
Perpendicular period resulted in the creation of such superb
fan vaultings as in St Andrew's, Cullompton, Devon.*

*Stone vaulting was too expensive for many churches,
but the use of cheaper timber could result in spectacular ceilings
like this at St Wendreda's, March, Cambridgeshire
with its flying angels.*

across the Channel because of the lower cost of water transport. But in the main, the church would be born, quite literally, of its locality. England possessing, as it does, a wide variety of geological strata, therefore has a correspondingly rich diversity of building stone, each presenting the mason with certain problems and certain advantages. Thus the hard granite of Cornwall demands monumental treatment with relatively little in the way of ornament — but as compensation is that fact that a 500 year old church looks as though the builders have only just taken down their scaffolding. In Norfolk, flint was there for the asking (even today local builders will refer to 'gathering flints' as though they were a crop). But though when 'knapped' it presents an almost jewel-like surface, ashlar is needed for corners. The prevalence of round towers in the area, where cut stone has proved too expensive to use, demonstrates its limitation.

In an earlier book, *The English Cathedral*, the present writer drew on modern researches to demolish the popular myth that there were no architects in the Middle Ages, that our great churches and cathedrals 'grew', as it were, organically: that, in the words of the scholar E S Prior in 1905:

'the function of architect as designer of buildings and determiner of its forms of beauty did not exist in any personality'.

The work of such historians of building as J H Harvey proves conclusively that the master mason effectively discharged the role of a modern architect. But this appears to have applied only to major projects. The paucity of church contracts quoted in L F Salzman's magisterial survey of medieval building techniques *Building in England* would seem to argue a large degree of spontaneity — that no one got around to making an overall contract because the work was done piecemeal with everyone taking a hand in it. The fact that measurements differed from village to village gives further evidence of the manner in which the local church literally grew out of the local community. The way in which the British have clung to their archaic mensuration, despite the half-hearted gesture towards the metric, gives us a vivid illustration of the sheer confusion of measurements reigning in medieval communities. The basic unit was the 'pole' of 16 feet (long since relegated to history, surviving still only in that deathless incantation — 'rod, pole, or perch'). This was arrived at in an entirely literal manner. Sixteen men were chosen at random and obliged to place their right feet one behind the other and their total length measured. A piece of wood, the pole itself, was cut to this measurement and became the village's standard unit. Half that pole was the yard but when this was shortened to 3 feet the pole itself was extended to 16 feet 6 inches.

The builders of cathedrals and the great churches belonged to the elite: men who travelled all over the country —and, indeed, all over Europe and were by no means illiterate. They had knowledge of, and even personal recourse to such seminal works as Vitruvius's *De Architectura*. Builders of the humble parish church largely worked literally by rule of thumb. One result of this ad hoc approach is today visible in many of our churches and gave rise to one of the numerous myths relating to them. Following that ancient division of responsibility between chancel and nave, whereby the vicar or rector was responsible for the former, and the laity the latter, there is frequently a marked difference in architectural style between the two. Sometimes a pious rector wanted to enlarge the chancel erected by a mean or penurious predecessor. On many an occasion, that new chancel was built at a distinct angle to the nave — producing the later myth that the builders intended this to represent Christ's head sagging to one side on the Cross.

Church finances in the early period would have been largely a matter of edict: the lord of the manor, whether secular or lay, simply decreeing that the work should be done and providing the finances for it. But as control over their church passed more and more into the hands of parishioners, so its funding became ever more complex, and the accounts of that funding provide a vivid side glance into the workings of everyday life. Most of these accounts related either to the rebuilding of an existing church, or the adding of some fashionably desirable feature by way of enhancement.

The accounts of the rebuilding of Bodmin church in Cornwall, between 1469 and 1472, survived in their entirety and show that this was a genuinely popular movement, with ordinary people contributing the equivalent of the widow's mite. A substantial part of the overall cost of £268 17s 9½d came from the established trade and religious guilds. Four of the trade guilds — the Millers, Cordwainers, Smiths and Skinners — contributed 'a penny per man of some and a halfpenny of others', the difference presumably reflecting the different status of members within the guild. The vicar himself contributed an entire year's salary. Some 460 individuals in the parish were listed as contributors, which must have included virtually every adult — and certainly every household. One 'hold woman' gave 3s 2½d. Exactly how many of these contributors were entirely spontaneous, and how many yielded under social pressure is rather open to doubt, bearing in mind one significant entry! 'Joachym Hoper is dead and nothing more can be got out of him'. Considerable quantities of gifts in kind were also recorded, ranging from the provision of building materials to provender for the builders.

At Long Melford in Suffolk, benefactors took care that their piety should be recorded in public as well as permanent form, and had their names inscribed on the exterior stonework, usually with the injunction to 'Pray for the sowle of . . . '. Northleach church in Gloucestershire has a number of handsome brasses commemorating the 'wool men' whose wealth created the superb Cotswold churches. On the other side of the country, the woolmen of East Anglia also poured their wealth into their churches. In Lincolnshire, John Lynwode specifically acknowledges his debt — and incidentally provides an illustration of the extensive area covered by these clothiers in quest of their raw material. Dying in 1410, he left £10 'to the thirty churches in whose parishes I was wont to buy wool'.

The handling of finances was the responsibility of the churchwardens and their meticulous and copious accounts, frequently detailing such minute sums as 4d for the hire of a horse for a warden sent to negotiate with a master mason, make up for the paucity of contracts. The usual pattern was for a village to engage a master mason from a town and agree a fee with him to exercise overall supervision. It would be his responsibility to hire skilled workmen, but they were paid direct by the wardens. A mixture of cash and kind was common. When the wardens of Walberswick church in Suffolk wanted to follow the fashion and add a tower to their church, they agreed to find all materials, provide lodgings for the masons, and pay them in addition to '40s of laugh-full money of Engelond', an annual barrel of herrings (a major product of this fishing town) and a warm gown for each mason annually. Payment was made by every yard of height, providing thereby both a means of measurement and a stimulus to the workmen. It required considerable organization on the part both of the wardens and their master mason to calculate when a particular kind of skill was needed — when, for instance, carpenters should take over from masons, or glaziers from carpenters. Even today, the building industry shows a pattern of ebb and flow as successive kinds of workers take over from each other. One of the mysteries of the medieval building industry is where these specialists came from and whence they disappeared after the work was done. In 1413, at Halstead in Essex, two carpenters, More and Taverner, were engaged to make a timber roof for the chancel. Before they could erect their roof masons had to raise the walls another 3 feet. Taverner's terms were that he should have the old roof timbers for his own use — by no means a trivial concession, for seasoned timber had a high value. The invaluable records of the rebuilding of Bodmin church provide a detailed account of what would today be called 'hours and conditions of labour'. An important town church of this nature could afford no fewer than three master masons — Richard Richowe and his two assistants John Hancock and Robert Wetter. Between them these three men controlled some 20 masons working either in the town or in the quarry on the moor. Here, the stone was not simply quarried, but all the dress and shaping done, the finished blocks being ready for use immediately they arrived on site. There seems to have been a considerable amount of freelance work: thus for a major project like building the south walls Richowe received £22 for himself 'and his fellowys' — that is, it became the master mason's responsibility to pay individual masons according to their status (a good mason got 6d a day). But on another occasion Richowe's assistant, Hancock, received a personal payment of 6d for pillars, windows and arch. Each mason had his personal mark — a fact which has given rise to much fanciful speculation as to their significance. It was simply the means whereby the master mason could calculate how much work a particular mason had performed over a period, Miscellaneous items in the Bodmin accounts include:

> 'parchmentes for to make rollys. [presumably for drafting purposes] 1d: 6 pairs of gloves for the carpenter, 6d: drink for John Hygowe and Losquit for brynging to the church a tree, 2d: and to John Andrew carrier yn drinke, 2d'.

The wardens were so anxious to have the work finished that they were even prepared to pay for candles both before and after Christmas when the masons' work would normally have ceased at sunset.

CHAPTER III

THE BUILDING

The characteristic feature of the English church, the feature which not only separates it from ordinary buildings, but also from most of its Continental brethren, is the soaring tower, frequently capped with a steeple. Even though they can be classified according to their period, the shape and size and position of towers is as varied, as idiosyncratic, as the churches they adorn. At one extreme is the soaring majesty of the ill-named Boston 'Stump'. Visible from a good 15 miles away across the flat Fenlands, it appears first as a vertical smudge. Unlike the towers of most urban churches, it does not disappear as one enters the town, coyly hiding behind adjacent buildings but, instead, emerges in its true shape as a graceful fretted lantern soaring high above its neighbours. Begun about 1430 – over a century after the church itself – taking some 90 years to build – it is some 302 feet high. The vast structure is quite hollow and at certain angles and at certain times of the day one can look right through it.

The Stump is, perhaps, the supreme example of the Perpendicular period – a period which excelled in tower-building. At the other extreme is the Saxon tower of Monkwearmouth in Tyne & Wear. Barely 60 feet high and 11 feet square it could be almost tucked into the bottom storey of the Stump, but measured against the low profile of the little church itself, it achieves considerable dignity.

Midway between these extremes comes a tower like that of Uffington church in Oxfordshire. Set squarely and solidly over the central crossing, its thirteenth century builders perhaps intended to erect a spire on its low octagonal base. If so, they never got round to it and it was left to the eighteenth century builders to add another storey.

The Georgians showed remarkable restraint in following the original solemn style, except for adding a frivolous crown of pinnacles and battlements.

*The Boston 'stump' soaring up like a
landed lighthouse in the flat Fenlands:
St Bartholomew, Boston, Lincolnshire.*

Saxon towers frequently discharged a defensive role. The tower of St Mary's in Guildford, Surrey, is unusual in that it was built before the church itself, probably as a watchtower. But defensive purposes depended as much upon geography as chronology: over three centuries after the tower of St Mary's had been incorporated into the church, as late as 1380, the squat, massive tower of Great Salkeld in Cumberland was built for purely military purposes. The battlements are real, not frivolous ornaments: the window slits present minimal breaks and the only entrance to the tower, from the nave, is through an iron-plated door. The tower is the product of a turbulent region, where cattle raiding was part of everyday life. Bedale church in Yorkshire carries the defensive concept even further, for the stairway to the tower was protected by a portcullis which was lowered when danger threatened and totally separated tower from nave.

In general, towers are a luxury intended simply to demonstrate the wealth and pride of its parish. Indeed, the builders of a tower were

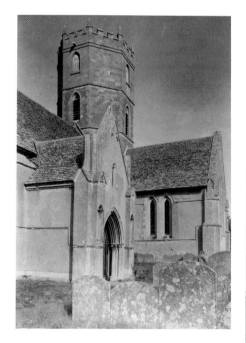

(Below) The Saxon love of display comes out clearly in the tower of All Saints, Earls Barton, Northamptonshire.

*(Above) The tower of St Mary's, Uffington, Berkshire.
The eighteenth century added a storey but forebore to embellish its austere form.*

frequently enjoined to copy that of a neighbouring and rival parish – but on a larger scale: thus the masons at Walberswick were told to follow the design of the tower at Tunstall. The tower of the great church of St Peter Mancroft in Norwich, Norfolk, was specifically intended to challenge the Boston Stump – but was never completed, doubtless to the chagrin of the churchwardens. The tower played no part in the liturgy and its architect was therefore free to indulge himself in its ornamentation, with some dramatic results. The massive tower of Earls Barton in Northamptonshire displays the Saxon love of crowded ornament. The rather squat structure is given an appearance of height and elegance by thin pilasters, linked by exuberant diamond and semicircular arcading.

But though each tower is absolutely individual, they fall into clear-cut groups, so that travelling across country one becomes very much aware of passing from one region into another simply by the design of the church tower. In East Anglia their buttresses tend to rise in a series of diminishing steps, like those of SS Peter and Paul in Lavenham. Somerset towers are famous for their exuberance, bursting out into pinnacles and pierced parapets and with large and handsome windows: Huish Episcopi's is an outstanding example. The towers of Surrey are plain and solid, Yorkshire's tend to the grand and solemn like St Mary's at Tickhill.

Having striven to overtop their neighbour's tower, many a parish went one step further and created the unique English contribution to

The tower of St Peter and St Paul, Lavenham, Suffolk shows the 'stepped' structure of the buttresses characteristic of East Anglia.

architecture, the spire. We tend to take them for granted but, as Olive Cook remarks: 'What a strange and original notion to build cloud-piercing needles of stone.' Spires are concentrated in Lincolnshire and the East Midlands. Considering the technical problems of placing hundreds of tons of stone on a base that was probably not built for such a purpose, they begin remarkably early, dating back to the mid-thirteenth century. At Louth in Lincolnshire the building of its great spire did not begin till 1501 – and some 15 years passed before the work was finished. The building records for this spire are unusually full, beginning in 1500 when a certain William Netlyton was hired to make 'trassyng and makyng molds' and continuing until the eve of Holy Rood in 1515 when the bells were rung for the first time and everyone present was given bread and ale. There must have been many times when the churchwardens must have regretted starting their ambitious project. The first master mason, John Cole, threw in his hand in 1506, apparently after a disagreement. Richard Scune, who took his place worked well for many years, then, not long before completion, he too departed in high dudgeon. Two men were sent to Boston to persuade him to come back (the hire of their horses cost 2 shillings) but he declined to do so and the long project was eventually completed by a John Tempas of Boston. The whole cost came to the immense total of £305 7s 4d and it is not clear how this small town raised such a sum.

The tower might be a luxury, but there was no reason why such a massive and expensive part of the building should not be put to use. Its most obvious use was that of a belfry. Bells played an important role in medieval life: not only summoning the faithful to church, but also at baptisms, festivals, and of course, funerals. They were the best means of informing the public of an emergency. From them developed the art of campanology unique to England. Change ringing was invented in 1668 by a Cambridge printer, Fabian Stedman, whose name has been immortalised in the 'Stedman peal'. A full peal of eight bells involves over 40,000 changes, a mistake in even one putting the whole sequence out. St Peter Mancroft in Norwich claims that the first recorded true peal took place there in 1715. Here the bells are housed separately from the ringers and the ringers' gallery usually has proudly displayed records of major peals, together with the rules governing the gallery.

The lower storey of the larger towers were frequently used as a school room, but undoubtedly the tower's most valuable social function was to act as lantern. Many a benighted traveller making his way through a pitch dark night in a strange country must have been grateful for the light in church tower. Leaving bequests for the

In the past, the church porch discharged a far more important role than it does today. No expense was spared to make the porch of St Mary's, Woodbridge, Suffolk, worthy of that role.

St Botolph, Boston, Lincolnshire.
The Boston 'Stump' as the tower is called is visible for
miles across the flat Fenland.

Holy Trinity, Bledlow, Buckinghamshire.

The Norman church of St Mary, Beverston, Gloucestershire.

maintenance of such a light was a common act of piety. Blakeney church on the coast of Norfolk actually has a miniature tower at its west end, of approximately the same height as the main tower, which was used as a lantern guiding seamen into the harbour immediately below. Boston Stump was also a lantern and the tower of All Saints Pavement in York is surmounted by a lantern intended to guide travellers through the forest of Galtre.

After the tower, the most distinctive external feature is the porch. Usually it was built on the south-western side and immediately faced the town. Occasionally it is found on the western side and known as a 'galilee', being the final station in a procession. In our own time, the porch has been downgraded in function to a mere appendage: a place to display church notices or perhaps a brightly decorated tree at Christmas. But originally, it had a function even more important than that of the nave. Certain parts of the mass were recited here. The preliminaries to baptism took place here, the sponsors making the responses before the child was carried – both literally and symbolically – into the church itself. Weddings took place here – did not Chaucer's indestructible Wife of Bath boast that 'husbands at churche dore had she five'. In some porches there are indications that they were even furnished with an altar: the Saxon church in Bradford-on-Avon, Wiltshire, whose immense porch is more than half the size of the nave, almost certainly had an altar. Much attention was lavished in this ceremonial entrance to the church: the unsuspecting visitor to Cirencester in Gloucestershire frequently takes the spectacular three storey porch of St John the Baptist's for the church itself. The abbots of Cirencester used it as their office for their wide-ranging secular interests. St Mary's in Woodbridge, Suffolk is finished in one of the country's finest examples of decorative flintwork, knapped flint and cut stone creating dazzling black and white patterns. The larger porches had an upper storey used for secular purposes. It was in the upper porch of Bodmin church in Cornwall that the building accounts were discovered in the nineteenth century and the tragic poet, Thomas Chatterton, found his inspiration in the upper room of the great porch of St Mary Redcliffe in Bristol.

Somewhere near the porch and usually on the south wall, will be found one of the most mysterious architectural details of the parish church: a small square window two or three feet above ground level. Usually it is described as the 'leper window' for it was supposed that lepers, forbidden to enter the church, stood in the churchyard and followed the Mass through the window. Few of these so-called 'leper windows' command a view of the altar and, in any case, lepers were rigorously excluded from the churchyard. It is possible that the function of the window was the prosaic one of providing ventilation.

At the east end of the church is the Lady Chapel. The cult of the Virgin Mary was virtually unknown before the twelfth century, but by the end of that century it had swept through the Church until it threatened to rival worship of the Trinity. Every parish who could afford it hastened to add a chapel to their church, choosing the nearest place to the high altar. The most spectacular of these is undoubtedly that at Long Melford in Suffolk. Built as late as 1496 it is virtually a separate building, totally different in plan and elevation from the rest of the church.

The great contribution made by the Perpendicular period to church architecture is the clerestory. This means of flooding the building with light was certainly not unknown in previous centuries. The thirteenth century church of West Walton in Norfolk has a majestic upper arcade surmounting the arcade of the nave, and St Margaret's in Cley-next-sea, also in Norfolk, has an enchanting series of lights – circular and rectangular – which have the rich mouldings of the

In St Edmund's, Southwold, Suffolk, window space has been increased so much that the walls have been reduced almost to the function of tracery.

Decorated period. But it is in the fifteenth century that the clerestory is fully developed. Sometimes it meant the expensive and complex business of raising the nave arcade by increasing the height of the piers, to accommodate it as at Spalding in Lincolnshire. Modern lighting systems have reduced the practical value of the clerestory, but one only has to compare the dim interior of a Saxon or early Norman church, with the light flooding into a fifteenth century church to appreciate what the clerestory must have meant to the parishioners of earlier centuries.

On entering the nave probably the first – and almost certainly the oldest – object upon which the visitor's gaze will alight, is the font. Sentiment and practical considerations together ensured that no matter how drastically a church might be rebuilt or extended, the sacred font would be retained. This massive, all but indestructible, object cost a great deal to produce and was also the tangible evidence of the parish church's most cherished right – that of baptizing its own parishioners. In the church of Pevensey, East Sussex, claimed to be the

The clerestory transformed the interior of a church, flooding it with light. In St Margaret's, Cley, Norfolk the clerestory windows are in the form of a cinquefoil within a roundel.

first church built by the Normans in England, the local children have produced a touching little guide book, drawing attention to, among other things, the 500 year old font 'where some of us were baptized'. A substantial number of fonts are early Norman, their large size indicating that total immersion was the usual practice for baptism before the thirteenth century. Norman fonts, such as those in Holy Trinity, Lenton, Nottinghamshire, and St Mary Magdalen, Eardisley, Hereford & Worcester, are richly carved, the surface crowded with figures and intricate interlacings reminiscent of Viking sculpture. In the fifteenth century the Seven Sacraments font came into fashion. This beautiful design seems to be peculiar to East Anglia – only two of the 38 in existence being found outside the region. The sculptor of the font in St Mary's Woodbridge, Suffolk was highly skilful in portraying a complex scene within the small scale of one of the eight panels. In the panel depicting the Sacrament of Baptism, for instance, he was able to show a priest receiving the infant from the godmother, while the godfather touches the child in a moving gesture of association. The panel showing Matrimony has been badly damaged by Puritan iconoclasts, presumably objecting to the ring being placed on the bride's finger. More understandably, the panel showing the Crucifixion has also been defaced.

In 1236 it was decreed that fonts should be provided with a locked cover to prevent the holy water being stolen for unhallowed purposes. From that injunction developed the extraordinary series of font covers which, again, found their apogee in East Anglia. In the church of St Mary, Ufford in Suffolk the cover is an immense, densely carved wooden object that reaches almost to the roof. It is made on the telescopic principle so that the base can be raised without disturbing the whole. Sudbury in Suffolk possesses a similar cover. Most of these creations were made by anonymous artists, but the church of All Hallows by the Tower of London, possesses a superb cover created by our foremost wood carver, Grinling Gibbons. Apart from the sheer versatility of the work, it is an interesting illustration of the thawing of the Puritan winter. Commissioned in 1682, it resolutely turns its back on the gloomy fanaticism which destroyed countless 'superstitious images' and is an enchanting cornucopia of fruit and flowers supported by light hearted little cherubs.

Standing with back to the font, the visitor faces what was one of the most important interior fittings of the church – the rood screen. It had at once a practical and a symbolic function: practical in that it separated the sacred area of the chancel from the secular nave, symbolic in that it signified the division between Heaven and Earth. It was called the 'rood' screen because it usually supported a large

The spectacular font cover in St Mary's, Ufford, Suffolk,
survived the attentions of the
Puritan iconoclast William Dowsing.

Thaw after the Puritan Winter:
a detail of Grinling Gibbons' elaborate font cover in
All Hallows Church, Tower Hill, London.

(sometimes life-size) figure of Christ on the Cross, or 'rood', flanked by the Virgin Mary and St John. By separating chancel from nave, making it physically difficult to see what was taking place at the high altar, the rood screen emphasized the difference between consecrated priest in whose hands alone lay the mystery of the sacrament, and the unconsecrated layman. Quite apart from its profusion of images, this concept of a division alone would have enraged the Puritans and rood screens came under particularly heavy attack from the iconoclasts. The oldest surviving screen in the country is that of St Michael's in Stanton Harcourt, Oxfordshire. Dating back to the thirteenth century, it is a plain wooden structure, the only ornamentation being the shape of the louvres in its upper half. Its plainness is unusual and points to its early date. The rood screen, in its dominant position and wide extent, was an ideal place upon which the wood carver could practice his skill. The fifteenth century screen in All Saints, Kenton, Devon, stretches the entire width of the nave. As with most screens it is in two parts, the lower a series of elegant arches supporting a row

The screen, separating clergy from laity, particularly aroused the ire of Puritan iconoclasts, and survivals such as this fifteenth century example in All Saints, Kenton, Devon are rare.

An even rarer example of a screen surviving the Puritan's destruction is this painted one in St Helen's, Ranworth, Norfolk.

of statues, each in its niche. Separating the two is a richly carved main beam, the bressumer. Above the rood screen was the rood loft. This had only a limited liturgical function, supporting perhaps a small organ and choir. It was also the means whereby the great figures on the rood screen could be covered in a pall during Lent. Most lofts fell victim to the Puritans, the only surviving evidence being the stone stairs which were usually built into an adjacent pillar.

Two features in the chancel which survived the iconoclasts, but now rarely have a function are the piscina and the sedilia. The piscina is simply a basin in which the priest ritually washed his hands and where the chalice used in the celebration of the Mass was also washed. According to the doctrine of transubstantiation, the consecrated wine in the chalice had become the actual blood of Christ. The cleansing of the chalice therefore presented a liturgical problem of high importance. As early as the ninth century it had been decreed that the water used to rinse the chalice and which, of its nature, must obtain a tincture of the consecrated wine, had to be disposed of in consecrated earth. The piscina discharged into the churchyard and so resolved this

*Like a frozen wave these
fourteenth century seats (sedilia), St Helen, Cliffe, Kent,
are for the officiating priest and acolytes.
The most distant niche is for the piscina where the
sacred vessels were washed.*

*A dramatic example of the Easter Sepulchre,
showing Christ rising from his tomb:
St Patrick's, Patrington, Humberside.*

problem. As with all other aspect of church architecture, what began simply became ever more complex. In the thirteenth century it became customary to provide a double piscina, one basin being used for the chalice and one for the washing of hands. With the changing of the liturgy, whereby the priest was required to drink the water used to rinse the chalice, this function of the piscina fell into disuse although it was still necessary to provide the means for the ritual washing of hands.

Near the piscina, and sometimes physically incorporated with it in the south wall of the chancel, are three large niches, one below the other. In the high Decorated period of the fourteenth century when the niches were richly sculptured, and connected with carved canopies, the three together descend the steps of the chancel like a frozen wave. The seats were for the celebrant, the deacon, and sub-deacon who sat in them at certain stages of the mass. Although three sedilia were the norm, the number can vary: The church at Ditchling in Sussex has only one, while the superb church of St Nicholas in Great Yarmouth, Norfolk, boasts no less than five.

Another physical survival which has now totally lost its function is the Easter sepulchre. Originally, its role was to play a part in that dramatic representation of the life of Christ which lay at the very heart of the medieval church. The Easter sepulchre symbolised the tomb of Christ, and on Good Friday the Blessed Sacrament was ritually placed in it, remaining there until Easter Sunday when it was removed to the high altar. During those three days it was watched over. Churchwardens' accounts frequently contained such references as that in the accounts of All Hallows on the Wall, London, for 1531 'for brede and drynke for them that wached the Sepucre, 1d'. Usually, the sepulchre was a moveable wooden structure and bequests for its embellishment was a popular gesture of piety. But some churches created elaborate stone structures of which that at St Patrick's in Partington, Humberside, is outstanding. Here the drama of the entombment and resurrection is given in concrete form. The sepulchre has three rectangular panels one above the other. The lowest panel shows the Roman soldiers asleep outside the tomb, the central panel has the triumphant Christ rising from a coffin, while the upper panel probably once showed the Ascension. For some reason this was the only panel destroyed by the iconoclasts. In the centre panel is the niche, complete with curtain, which held the consecrated wafer.

CHAPTER IV

AD MAJOREM DEI GLORIAM

The nineteenth century enthusiasm for all things medieval revived the resounding phrase '*Ad majorem Dei gloriam*' (to the greater glory of God) inscribing it, in what appears to be almost an afterthought, on the bottom of many a gaudy window celebrating some local worthy. The term had a far wider meaning however. It could be applied to the endless hours a monk might spend illuminating the initial letter of a manuscript, or to the ornamentation of the church that transformed a stone shell into the equivalent of an illuminated manuscript.

Far more than in its two related religions, symbolism dominated the architecture of Christendom, an expression of the medieval attempt to render tangible the intangible, an attempt which ranges from the doctrine of transubstantiation, to the rendering of the third person of the Trinity in the form of a bird. The Gothic revival of the nineteenth century, in the unquestioning adulation of the medievel mind, took that passion for symbolism to absurd lengths, arguing that it applied to the very form of the church:

> 'Because of the religion of Christ Crucified is preached in their walls, a vast number of our churches have been constructed on the cross form. . . To signify the Holy Trinity, we have the threefold division of a church into nave, transepts and choir'.

Alec Clifton-Taylor cites a guide book in a Shropshire church which solemnly informs its readers that:

> 'the inner walls (of the church) are sloping and curved at the west end like a ship, being symbolic of the Ark while the main aisle has a definite slope from the west up to the altar, symbolic of the ascent to Calvary'.

Such aberrations in the form of the church were due to the *ad hoc* system of measurements, while the deliberate cruciform shape is, on the whole unusual rather than common. It was in the ornamentation of the church, not its structure, that symbolism found expression. Intended for a congregation which could not read, the bewildering richness of symbolism is today largely incomprehensible to the non specialist. Much of it derives from biblical stories and allegories – Noah's Ark, the Lamb, the keys of heaven – which still retain their significance for a modern audience. The woodcarver, though, who created the exquisite little sculptures on the seats of misericords or the mason who followed his fancy in some obscure corner of the church, crowding the surface of his material with an exuberant rampaging of wild life, was using as a guide, the medieval bestiary which sought to endow various animals with certain fanciful characteristics. Thus the hedgehog signifies the Devil for he impales human souls in the same way that the hedgehog supposedly impales grapes on his spine. The lion is typecast as Christ himself in his role of judge; the unicorn as a symbol of virginity.

The interior of most of our churches today bear a sober – not to say frequently sombre – appearance with walls of naked brick or stone or at best, whitewashed. A medieval church in its heyday would, to our eyes, have appeared to have an almost fairground gaudiness, with the carvings of the woodwork picked out in a blaze of gold and red and green and the walls liberally covered with murals. Opposite the door is frequently an immense painting of St Christopher carrying the Christ child. The saint is one of those (along with St Philomena and St George) who have fallen victim to twentieth century academic scepticism. He never existed. But for generations he was regarded as the patron saint of travellers and thus welcomed them into the church. Little Missenden church in Buckinghamshire, has an almost perfect representation of the legend and in the riot of wall painting on Pickering church in Yorkshire, the giant figure of the saint is shown striding out. Usually, he is shown, with Christ on his back and a knobbly staff in his hand, wading through a shallow stream.

After St Christopher, the 'Doom' was one of the most popular of all murals. Over a hundred of these have survived, the oldest being in Patcham church, Sussex, which dated back to the late twelfth century. The fact that, like most such murals, it was covered in whitewash by the Puritans probably contributed to its survival. The restorers in 1880 uncovered no less than 30 coats. Most Dooms were painted at the east end of the church so that the worshipper, striving perhaps to keep awake, had the opportunity to contemplate one or other of the fates open to him after death. The great 'Doom' in St Thomas's church in

The doom mural at St Peter and St Paul, Chaldon, Surrey.

Salisbury tells the conventional story. Christ is shown seated on a rainbow in the centre, flanked by his Apostles. Far below them on the left, the dead are rising from their graves, while on the right of the arch the damned are being driven into the mouth of a monster. Although the colours now appear sombre, they were probably much brighter, and the draughtsmanship is of a high order. The extraordinary 'Ladder of Salvation' in Chaldon, Surrey uses a different subject to thrust home the same point but with inferior technique. About the same period as the Patcham Doom it is composed of two panels one above the other, linked by a ladder up which tiny naked figures are desperately scrambling to escape the horrors of hell in the lower panel. As with all such eschatological paintings, the horrors of hell offer far more scope than the insipid pleasures of heaven, and the artist has indulged himself to the full, not only creating an ingenious series of torments administered by monsters in hell, but even bringing these lively monsters into the heaven panel where one supervises the weighing of souls with the archangel, and another stands in for Satan in Christ's harrowing of hell.

Most church murals are, of their nature, religious, but the twelfth century church in Pyrford, Surrey, has a crude secular sequence which, discovered only in 1967, is so far believed to be unique in the country. The discovery illustrates both the extreme vulnerability of murals, hence their relative rarity, and the fact that one generation will quite happily paint over the work of a previous one, for all the world like suburban householders covering the wall-paper of their predecessor with one of their own choice. The south wall of the Pyrford church contains fragments of a mural, dated around 1200, with the conventional subject of the 'Flagellation of Christ'. It was deteriorating badly and a decision was made to restore it. Beneath it, however, a fresco dating from some sixty years earlier was discovered, probably contemporary with the building of the church. It is in red ochre and shows a number of tiny warriors, both mounted and on foot, with a boat containing other armed men. Given that this extraordinary scene was painted some seventy years after the Norman Conquest, is it an attempt to record, belatedly, that famous victory in a church built by the conquerors or does it show a contemporary, local action? The narrow but navigable River Wey runs not far away and the boat containing soldiers could conceivably be on a riverine expedition.

Even without the attention of the iconoclasts, murals were vulnerable. Few are genuine frescoes – that is, painted while the plaster is still wet and so becoming an integral part of it. Painted 'dry' they simply rubbed off when the surface of the plaster deteriorated. Damp affected them: if the plaster had to be renewed the frescoes were simply chipped away. They could also fall victim to changing fashion as the Pyrford mural. One or two are from the hands of a true master. The thirteenth century 'Virgin and Child' in St Mary's, Canfield, Essex is the equal of any contemporary manuscript illumination. In the main, however, they seem to have been the work of jobbing painters using cheap materials – red and yellow ochre for the most part – rather than what today we would term 'artists'.

The painters of such timber artefacts as the rood screen or the reredos or the roof were undoubtedly artists. Their work was expected to last: they were paid at a far higher rate than the woodcarvers and the sums involved were substantial. Thus the churchwardens of St Edmund's in Salisbury, Wiltshire, paid a John Coleyn £16 in 1497 'for the painting of the rood with Mary and John and for gilding the figures with stars'. The high prices reflected the costs of materials rather than the status of the painter. Gold leaf was lavishly used for gilding and the best quality of the blue or 'azure' (obligatory for the Virgin's costume) was actually made from lapis lazuli. Very few churches could afford such luxury and a blue known as 'azure biz' costing about a quarter of the price of lapis lazuli was widely used. A vibrant red could be obtained by using red lead, green was obtained from verdigris, and 'indigo of Baghdad' was popular.

Despite their artistic level, despite the intrinsic value of their materials, paintings on timber in churches proved little less vulnerable than those on walls. Their destruction was less due to religious fanaticism than the passion for 'restoration' in the eighteenth and nineteenth centuries. In the eighteenth century, in particular, roodscreens, whose bases made perfect media for panel paintings, were swept away in the passion for opening up the church. Sometimes the destruction arose out of sheer ignorance. Thomas Hardy, a founding member of the Society for the Protection of Ancient Buildings tells the story of a church whose restoration had been placed under his supervision:

> 'There was an old oak screen, very valuable with the original colouring and gilding, though much faded. The repairs deemed necessary had been duly specified, but I beheld in its place a new screen of deal. "Well", said the builder genially, "I said to myself now I'm about it, I'll do the thing well, cost what it will". "Where's the old screen", I said appalled. "Used to boil the workmen's kittles – though 'a were not much at that".'

Those screens which survived the ignorant vandalism of the 'restorers' only too often fell victim to the more sophisticated vandalism of the collector. St Mary at Thornham Parva in Suffolk has the fourteenth century panel of a retable which has been compared to contemporary Sienese painting. The central panel is that of a Crucifixion, conventional in its layout with Christ flanked by the Virgin and St John. But the grieving figures have a grace of form and profundity of expression that makes them fit observers of the awesome event. At some period the retable disappeared from the church, and was actually discovered at an auction sale, complete with lot mark. Due to the lottery of time some survived unscathed to give an indication of the scale of our loss. The richly painted lower half of the rood screen at Ranworth in Norfolk survives in its entirety with the row of solemn witnesses to the faith, each in his niche – an outstanding work in a region of outstanding paintings. The artform which is more characteristic, more evident than any other is the stained glass which turns the humblest church into a glowing gem. Curiously, although the English were perfectly well acquainted with the techniques of producing glass, and had been using plain greenish-white glass in windows since the early thirteenth century, production of coloured glass did not become nationally established until the sixteenth century. The bulk of coloured glass before that period – in particular the glass of the thirteenth and fourteenth centuries which is now generally recognised as achieving the peak of the art – was imported from the

The nave of St Mary, Beverston, Gloucestershire.

St Laurence, Ludlow, Shropshire,
contains a superb sequence of misericords.

continent. The gap in development is all the more curious when it is considered that the essentially English style of Perpendicular, with its immense window openings, allowed the church to be turned into a kind of crystal palace where the stone tracery seems little more obtrusive than the leaden strips in the windows, creating the impression of towering walls of galls. Glass-makers of France and Germany were able to produce an astonishing range of colours by introducing metals into the molten glass: the rich ruby so popular with the glaziers was produced by copper oxide, purple was produced by manganese, blue by cobalt oxide, and various shades of yellow and green were the product of iron oxide. A beautiful, warm yellow ranging from lemon to orange, was first produced in the fourteenth century and was obtained by painting glass with a solution of silver sulphide and then firing it, the final shade of colour dictated by the temperature at which the glass was fired. The yellow added life to many a 'portrait', for it was widely used to provide hair, beards for men, and haloes for both sexes of saints. The actual window was built up like a jigsaw. The completed pattern was laid on a bench with lines marked to indicate the shapes of the glass pieces. These were then cut to size and placed over the drawing. In the earlier period, the leads which held the pieces together were regarded as a necessary evil and made as unobtrusive as possible. But later the dramatic possibility of these bold lines of black against the blazing window was fully exploited.

Considering the highly vulnerable nature of glass, liable to chemical deterioration as well as the hazard of shattering, a surprising quantity of glass from the fourteenth century onwards has survived. The most complete set of windows is in the church of St Mary in Fairford, Gloucestershire. The twenty-eight windows date from the late fifteenth century and are of interest not only in themselves, but they demonstrate how the iconography of churches was not done on an *ad hoc* basis but according to a well-thought out programme. The ornaments of a church, whether carvings or painting, were intended as much to instruct as to decorate. At Fairford, the windows of the Lady Chapel tell the Old Testament story up to the birth of Christ. The chancel, where the sacrifice of the mass took place, is logically devoted to the 'Passion of Christ'. 'The Resurrection' is, again logically, at the east end of the south nave, while the Apostles, early saints, and martyrs each have their due place in the sacred sequence.

One of the most moving, because the most spontaneous, graphic representations in a church, is the work of the graffiti 'artists'. Such activities today would undoubtedly arouse disapproval and, probably, the intervention of the law. But the thousands of such marks which have come down over the centuries throw a fitful but authentic light on the life of that most elusive person in history, the ordinary man. The most common of these marks are the so-called 'mason's marks' – those used by a mason to identify his work. They are fairly elaborate geometric designs, each was individual – and quite often handed down, slightly modified, to a son. The fact that their use could be so controlled is a lively demonstration of the close-knit and well-run nature of the masons' guild. The marks are not found upon the more elaborate pieces of stonework such as sculpture or any form of ornamentation, for such work would have been easily identified as the product of a particular craftsman. The mason's mark was usually related to ordinary stonework in order to assist the calculation of how much work had been done by a particular man. By collating these marks it is possible to follow not only the progress of a mason in a large church, but even follow him around the country. On some of the more elaborate pieces of stonework a mason might record his name and date out of justifiable pride of work. At Berden church in Essex, a mason signed his name near the chancel arch GEFRAI LIMATHUM (Geoffrey the Mason). Ropsley Church in Lincolnshire has a remarkably lengthy inscription in Latin *Ista columna facta fuit ad festum Sancti Michaelis anno domini MCCCLXXX et nomen factoris Thomas Bate de Corby*, This column was made on the Feast of St Michael AD

The most famous graffiti of all: the cry of despair brought on by the Black Death: St Mary's, Ashwell, Hertfordshire.

1380 and the maker's name is Thomas Bate of Corby). Did Thomas Bate get a clerk to provide him with the inscription or was he as adept in Latin as he was in stone? The latter is by no means improbable: there are a number of such lengthy Latin inscriptions in existence. Perhaps the most famous is that in Ashwell Church, Hertfordshire, which recording the ravages of the Black Death, can be translated as: 1350. Wretched, wild and distracted. The dregs of people survive as witnesses [of the plague] and in the end a tempest. This year S. Maur thunders on the earth. 1361.' There was, in fact, a tremendous storm on January 15 (St Maur's Day) 1361 which caused so much damage to the church that both nave and tower had to be substantially rebuilt. It may be that the unusual number of graffiti in the church, which were probably made by professional masons, were produced during this rebuilding. Near the Black Death inscription is a detailed representation of a large church which is believed to have been Old St Paul's Cathedral and may have been inscribed by the masons who rebuilt the church tower. On the tower itself is a casually scratched list of wages and materials, while on the nave piers are a number of most curious comments and adjurations, all in Latin of varying degrees of accuracy:

'The corners [of a piece of masonry] badly joined: I spit at them
. . .Drunkeness destroys whatever wisdom touches.'

A representation of Old St Paul's cathedral, London: graffiti on the tower wall of St Mary's, Ashwell, Hertfordshire.

In the 1970s a husband and wife team, Herbert and Barbara Rusbridger, began recording some of the thousands of apparently unrelated scratchings that appear throughout our older churches. Their recording technique was of the simplest: graphite with a little bicycle oil as binding agent on a soft chamois leather pad, a device which was not only cheap and effective but does no harm compared with the friction created by rubbing. In all, they visited over 1,300 churches and made 3,000 copies. It was in the classifying of the scores of symbols that a coherent story began to appear. A crudely scrawled symbol that looked like a 'W' but was believed to have been a linked 'V V' was so widespread that they gave up recording it. A probable interpretation is *Ver Vinces* – the truth shall conquer – scratched by Catholics at the time of persecution. Whereas, today graffiti and obscenity tend to be synonymous, the Rusbridgers found only one obscenity among the thousands of graffiti they recorded. Early examples were either symbolic or religious. Both died away with the sixteenth century and thereafter the graffiti became less interesting with an increasing number of formalized designs including the person's initials – the kind of thing common in our own time. The Rusbridgers made the excellent point that these scratches really are contemporary history as recorded by the man in the street and the cruder they were, the more likely they were to be authentic. Thus Tudor costume was formalized as broad shouldered and tight waisted with a flowing skirt like an appendage. Accident, time, chance, have all placed marks over the originals:

> 'We were driven mad by men who sharpened their arrows or spears by drawing them up and down on the stone, making deep incisions.'

It takes a careful and trained eye to spot these communications from the past. In the twelfth century church of Compton in Surrey, is a well known graffiti carefully preserved behind perspex. Receiving permission to rub it, Barbara and Herbert Rusbridger obtained the representation of a fourteenth century bishop. The churchwarden was astonished, 'I've sat by that stone every Sunday for 25 years and never seen that bishop'.

The same man in the street view of life as that provided by the graffiti, though one executed with conscious art and paid for, can be found in the carvings under the misericords – the tip-up seats in the stalls of chancels. These exquisite little carvings rarely have a religious significance, on the contrary, their subjects are usually not only secular and mythological but quite often of an earthiness which verges on the obscene and frequently involve a savage attack on the clergy. In St Botolph's church in Boston, Lincolnshire a fox dressed as an abbot is reading from a book, held up by a donkey, to an audience of five hens and a cock. The carvers of misericords showed very great skill in creating entire vignettes in small, arbitrarily defined areas. In the superb sequence at Ludlow in Shropshire is a mermaid admiring herself in a glass, flanked by two ferocious dolphins. Swinbrook in Oxfordshire has the somewhat disturbing upper half of a man seemingly emerging from the woodwork. Curiously, these carvings survived the age of the iconoclasts, whereas genuinely religious representations fell victim.

Misericords are mostly found in the great town churches or those which had been associated with some collegiate or monastic foundation. More widely spread are the elaborately carved bench ends. The earliest surviving benches in the country are those in Clapton-in-Gordano in Somerset, dating back to the fourteenth century. These earlier benches are massive and dignified, but quite plain, whereas those dating from the fourteenth and fifteenth centuries seem to burst out in an astonishing flowering of design: some abstract, but many following the lead of the misericords and depicting complete scenes within the rectangular shape. At Brent Knoll in Somerset, the attack on the clergy takes extreme and remarkable form. As with the St Botolph misericord, a fox dressed as an abbot is preaching to an animal audience – three pigs in cowls (presumably meant to be monks) and parishioners in the form of geese. The caricature does not end here, for successive bench ends show the fox, still in his sacerdotal dress, in the stocks, and finally hanging on a gallows. Dearly one would like to know who paid for these carvings and how permission was obtained to erect them in the church. The mysterious Green Man appears in Lansaalos, Cornwall, but unlike the misericords, there are also conventional religious themes. Blythburgh in Suffolk has a lively series of the 'Seven Deadly Sins', carved in the last quarter of the sixteenth century. Here, again, the wood carver has achieved a miracle of compression somewhat reminiscent of the Japanese netsuke, where spirited action is taking place in the most limited of areas. The Suffolk wood carver created his miniature scenes in the finial of the bench end – a piece of wood about the size of a human fist. Drunkeness expiates his sin in the stocks, Sloth is actually portrayed in bed, Avarice sits on a money chest, Pride is portrayed in fashionable costume. Other bench ends show the activities of the seasons: a pig is being killed in winter: a sower casts seed in spring: summer shows a harvester binding a sheaf of corn: autumn rather curiously repeats the idea with a reaper, instead of the usual cornucopia of fruit.

*(Above and opposite) Misericords in St Lawrence's,
Ludlow, Shropshire.*

There is one other aspect of *Ad Majorem Dei Gloiram* which takes the whole subject abruptly into the realm of metaphysics for it is the dedication, not of a work of art, but of an actual human being to the church. Although usually referred to as an 'anchorite', the person who voluntarily became immured in a tiny cell attached to the church seems to have been usually a woman – an anchoress. The cell was normally built on the north or colder and darker side of the church as an additional penance. It was a single-story structure, with a small opening on the outside to allow pilgrims to receive the blessing of the inmate without entering the church, and for the inmate to receive the necessities of life. Inside there was a 'squint' through which the occupant could follow the ceremonies taking place at the altar. In most cells there was no exit. The occupant was walled up as irrevocably as any sinning vestal virgin in her living tomb, the main difference being that the anchorite would spend years, rather than hours, under these conditions. Few cells survive, partly because they were relatively flimsy structures, merely attached to a church rather than an integral part of it, and after the death of the occupant there was little incentive to maintain it. But also, perhaps, their destruction came about because of the genuine abhorrence felt by later generations towards this extraordinary self-immolation. The Norman church of Shere in Surrey has the indications of such a cell in its north side. It is told that the anchoress, a young girl, unsurprisingly regretted her decision after the first few weeks of religious euphoria and somehow contrived to escape. She was recaptured and forcibly immured to scream out the short remainder of her life.

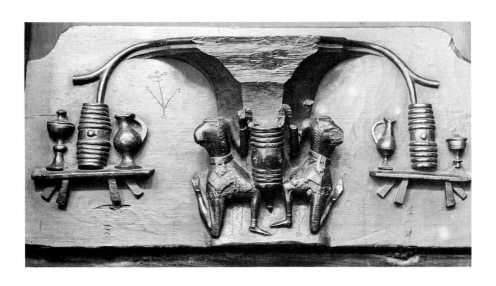

*Anti-clerical legends of the Fox on bench ends in
St Michael's, Brent Knoll, Somerset.(Above) The Fox as bishop.
(Right)The Fox imprisoned in the stocks, his mitre removed.
(Far Right) The Fox hung.*

She was probably an exception. The few contemporary accounts of medieval anchorites indicate that they perfectly adapted to their circumstances and became objects of considerable veneration – so venerated, indeed, that in one case the memory of an anchoress was sufficient to bring about the restoration of a not particularly distinguished church after its destruction by air raid in World War II.

St Julian's church in Norwich, Norfolk, was founded some time in the tenth century. Burnt by the Danes, it was rebuilt by the Normans and over the following centuries adapted in the usual manner but never achieved any great architectural merit. In the fourteenth century an anchorite cell was built for a woman about whom we know nothing personal apart from her sex and the fact that she was 36 years old on 8 May 1373. Even the name by which she is generally known, 'Dame Julian' is taken from the name of the church and not *vice versa* as is commonly supposed. On that May night she came near to death by illness and had a series of sixteen visions, which she calls 'shewings', relating to the passion of Christ. She describes them, quite undramatically and factually in a manner which, to a twentieth century reader, seems rather like the description of a series of cinema stills. Recovering, she meditated on them for some 20 years before writing her *Revelations of Divine Love*, one of the great works of metaphysical literature and, probably, the world's first prose work written by a woman. Her fame spread. Her cell became a place of national pilgrimage until her death some time in the fifteenth century.

In due course, the area in which the church was situated, together with the church itself, descended rapidly in the social scale. In the late nineteenth century there was even a proposal to demolish it, and its destruction by fire in 1941 seemed to have brought its long life to a natural term. Far from there being any incentive to restore a shabby and architecturally undistinguished church in an unfashionable area, the city of Norwich was wrestling with the problem of what to do with the many superb, but now functionless, churches in the old city centre. Nevertheless, the fame of 'Dame Julian', based on her book, was sufficient to bring about the rebuilding of the fire-gutted church. Her original cell had been demolished in the sixteenth century, but fragments of flint foundation showed its probable site and dimensions, allowing a reconstruction that probably approximates closely to the original. As with all such cells, there is a squint allowing a view of the altar and a large opening (now a four-light window) on the outside wall which overlooks what used to be a lane or road. There is no ceiling to the cell, the steeply slanting roof coming down to walls

*St Julian's, Norwich. Gutted by fire during World War II,
the post-war rebuilding revealed the outline of 'Mother Julian's' cell,
and it was rebuilt.*

*St Julian's, Norwich. The interior of 'Mother Julian's' cell,
now rebuilt and a focus of pilgrimage.*

about 5 feet high. But the overall dimensions are by no means
oppressive and there is, in addition, a doorway leading into the nave
of the church. Unlike the tragic anchoress of Shere 'Dame Julian' was
probably never immured, kept her sanity thereby, and created her
undying work. Her cell is now a chapel, focal point not simply of
national, but international pilgrimages.

CHAPTER V

THE TREASURE HOUSE

The interior of a much loved parish church rather resembles the attic of a large family house where cherished objects are stored long after they have ceased to have any function. The number and variety of these objects preserved in the church reflect the variety of roles played by a building which, for centuries, was not only the community's social centre, but was probably the only building that offered physical security and shelter for corporate activities. Here was the community's safe deposit in the form of the parish chest where wills and other vital records were kept. Here, money was collected for the poor and passed on to them in the form of doles in cash or kind. Here was the school room and, frequently, the council chamber. Here the city or town guilds held their services and recorded their existence. All these activities leave some trace, tangible in artefact or intangible in history. Chilham church in Kent preserves an immense table which was used by school children when a school was held in the priest's room over the south porch. The table is covered with carved initials, the oldest dated 1753. Blythburgh in Suffolk has a massive alms box dating back to 1473 – and still in use. In 1965 the lock was reinforced with a pair of handcuffs after being damaged during a theft. Chester's church of St John has a mace board in the Lady Chapel containing a list of all mayors who lived in the parish. Stokesay in Shropshire has a mounting block from the time when parishioners of this widely scattered parish rode to church.

The Christian belief that it was possible to assist the passage of a soul from purgatory to heaven by the means of prayer created one of the most selfish, and one of the most beautiful features of larger churches from the thirteenth century onward. This was the 'chantry chapel', virtually a church within a church, with its own altar, its own priest and, most important of all, its own endowment. A rich man

St Nicholas's Church, Arundel: monument to the seventh Earl of Arundel and his wife in the Fitzalan Chapel, which is independent of the church itself.

would leave in his will sufficient money not only to build the chapel, but to ensure that, for all eternity, a mass would be sung there on his behalf. The chapel would therefore be equipped with everything necessary from vestments to altar furnishings. Despite the Statute of Mortmain, passed in 1289, which, among other measures purported to control the proliferation of chantries, the numbers increased spectacularly during the thirteenth and fourteenth centuries, affecting the actual shape of churches. Thus the church of St John the Baptist in Cirencester, Gloucestershire is almost as broad as it is wide for it expanded steadily to accommodate the increasing number of chantries. As the cult spread so ordinary people joined in, combining in guilds or other associations to create chantries for corporate use. In Cirencester, two knights combined to endow a chantry on behalf of the wool guild: the brass of one of the chantry priests is still to be seen in the chapel. The church of St Michael in Coventry, Warwickshire had seven guild chapels at Cirencester. Many of these chapels were relatively simple wooden structures, destined to be swept away by the fervour of the Reformation, but the stone built ones survived. The

Ducal splendour: the Fitzalan Chapel in Arundel Castle, Sussex.

church of St Mary Magdalen in Newark, Nottinghamshire has two exquisite stone built chapels, one on each side of the altar, erected by the Meyring and Markham families in 1500 and 1508 respectively.

Tucked in a corner of Holy Trinity Church at Stow Bardolph in Norfolk is a flimsy looking cupboard. It looks as though it might contain spare hymnals or a brush and dustpan, but the unsuspecting visitor who opens the cupboard is in for a shock – in it is the upper half of a woman, a rather formidable woman in late middle age. It takes a split second for the mind to realize that this is an effigy, so horribly life-like is it. The figure is made of wax – one reason for its realism – and is Sarah Hare, from a prominent local family. She pricked her finger while doing needlework and died of blood poisoning in 1744. But she had already made arrangements for this strange memorial, not only sitting for the portrait, but leaving ringlets of her own hair, together with her own white dress and red cloak to adorn it.

Of all the features of a church the funerary monument is the most poignant, appealing to the widest possible range of people. The ordinary layman recognizes his predecessor across the gap of time and death, recognition often made explicit with a carved skull and some variation of the mocking phrase 'Today me: tomorrow you'. The genealogist finds here perhaps the last links in a chain: in the eighteenth century in particular, the recital of the deceased's virtues, offices, and antecedents fills large areas of marble. The social historian in quest of costume details, the artist in quest of inspiration, the moralist in search of a text, all find here material for their purpose.

Unlike so much else in the church, the funerary monument bridges the great divide of the Reformation, produced as lavishly after the sixteenth century as before. At first bewildering in their variety, each by definition unique, church monuments fall into a series of clear-cut classes. If one could film a sequence of monuments from the thirteenth to the late eighteenth centuries one would see, in effect, the effigy of the deceased slowly rising from a supine position on a coffin slab in the twelfth century, to the fully upright position of the eighteenth and nineteenth centuries, with an intermediate stage in the sixteenth century, when the effigy reclines with an air of insouciance upon one elbow. Curiously, it is the earlier period – the so-called Age of Faith – which lays emphasis on the purely physical aspect of death, showing the decomposing body in a number of forms, like the wasted cadaver of Sir John Golafre, who died in 1442, and whose monument is in Fyfield, Berkshire. It is the supposedly rational eighteenth and nineteenth centuries which speak of the glories of the Resurrection, with such monuments as that of Henrietta, Countess de Grey, in the church of Flitton Bedfordshire. She died in 1848 and her elaborate

*(Above) The curiously disturbing monument of
Sir Oliver de Ingham (d. 1344)
in Holy Trinity, Ingham, Norfolk.*

*(Right) Monument to Thomas Farnham (d. 1500)
in St Bartholomew's, Quorndon, Leicestershire.*

monument shows her being borne aloft by an angel. The seventeenth century contributes a link between the macabre realism of the Middle Ages and the optimistic symbolism of the later period by combining skull and wings as symbol of life after death.

Funerary monuments begin with the Normans. At first they were nothing more than the stone slab covering the coffin with a cross engraved upon it and, perhaps, some indication of the profession of the deceased – a sword for a knight or a chalice for a priest. By the end of the twelfth century the fully engraved figure of the occupant began to appear. Almost invariably, these would have been on high ecclesi-

Companions through eternity: monument to
Sir Richard Vernon (d. 1451) and his wife Lady Margaret,
in St Bartholomew's, Tong, Shropshire.

astics and were usually limited to the greater churches and cathedrals. In the early thirteenth century full, life-size effigies began to appear. Usually, these were placed on top of 'table tombs' – the large, box-like structures whose exteriors were frequently carved with armorial bearings. It is now that knights begin to take over from ecclesiastics, reflecting perhaps the steady swing towards secularization already evident in the patronage of the churches themselves. The most famous, and certainly the oldest sequence of these knightly effigies, is that in the Temple church in London. Their survival is nothing short of miraculous. Long since moved from their original tombs and placed on the floor of the round, as the oldest part of the church is known from its shape, they came close to total destruction when the Temple was gutted by fire during the London blitz. Remarkably restored, they lie again at the feet of visitors, staring up at the rood in curiously contorted positions. Among them are William Marshall, Earl of Pembroke, 'last of the feudal barons', who died in 1219 and his two sons and, wearing a great cylindrical helmet, the brutal Geoffrey de Mandeville, Earl of Essex who terrorized East Anglia in the reign of Stephen. Some of the knights have their legs crossed while in the act of drawing a sword and it has been argued – though without conclusive proof – that this denotes their status as Crusaders. The curious 'heart' monument which appears in some churches is undoubtedly linked to the overseas death of the deceased, the body being buried at the place of death and the heart brought home for interment in his church. Usually, these monuments relate to soldiers – for obvious reasons – but the monument in Yaxley, Huntingdonshire, commemorates an abbot, William Yaxley of Thorney. A heart-shaped object is shown being held up by two hands: remains of the heart were found in 1842 inside a box in a cavity behind the stone.

Female effigies began to appear only a generation or so after the first male figures. One of the earliest of these is the majestic lady in Wolferlow church, Herefordshire, haughtily occupying her own tomb slab about the year 1250. But that love could grow out of arranged marriages is again and again made evident by such touching monuments as that of Sir William and Lady Wilcote in Northleigh church, Oxfordshire. Sir William died in 1410, his wife presumably some time afterwards, but they lie serenely side by side, their right hands joined together. In South Stoke church in Lincolnshire, a fourteenth century knight and his lady lie cosily together under a single blanket. Alice, Duchess of Suffolk, who died in 1475, had herself portrayed in widow's weeds. With the sixteenth century, family relationships become ever more emphasized, with the children of the deceased ranged on the tomb chest beneath them, girls under

*St Martin's, Stamford, Lincolnshire: The tomb of the great
William Cecil, Lord Burghley, Treasurer to Elizabeth I, is here in the
church and not in the chapel of his splendid house nearby.*

the mother, boys under the father, neatly arranged by size.

In the early nineteenth century Richard Rush, an ambassador to England of the infant American republic, put his finger on one of the strengths of the English aristocracy, one of the factors which had enabled them to survive when their European counterparts were crashing in ruin. It was because they were rooted in the country, he thought:

> 'They have *houses* in London in which they stay while Parliament sits . . . but their *homes* are in the country. Their turreted mansions are there with all that denotes perpetuity – heirlooms, family memorials, pictures, tombs . . . '

Rush could have thrust his point home even further by remarking that the family mausoleum was rarely in the 'turreted mansion' but far more likely was in the parish church, emphasizing the family's link with the locality. Thus the memorial to Lord Burghley, Lord High Treasurer of England, confidant of Elizabeth I, is not in the splendid house which Daniel Defoe likened to a town, but in the parish church of Stamford, Lincolnshire, at the gates to the great park. Warwick the Kingmaker rests in the superb Beauchamp chapel of St Mary's in Warwick along with Ambrose Dudley, Earl of Warwick and his brother Robert, Earl of Leicester. Over the effigy of the Kingmaker – an effigy with its gaze calmly directed at the mural of the 'Madonna and Child' on the distant wall – is still the 'hearse', the metal frame

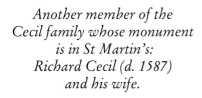

Another member of the Cecil family whose monument is in St Martin's: Richard Cecil (d. 1587) and his wife.

*The Beauchamp Chapel in St Mary's, Warwick:
the tomb in the foreground has a 'hearse' (used for bearing the pall)
over the effigy.*

work which once carried the pall. Amersham church in Buckingham-shire has the grandiose monuments of the Drake family, local squires for over 300 years. Bottesford church in Leicestershire has probably the oldest and longest range of aristocratic memorials – the tombs of the owners of nearby Belvoir Castle. The oldest of these is the diminutive effigy of Robert de Roos who died in 1285, showing the knight in full armour, and the sequence continues on to that of John, eighth Earl of Rutland who died in 1679. The tomb of Francis, the sixth earl (died 1632) bears an inscription claiming that his two sons 'dyed in their infancy by wicked practice and sorcery'. The inscription was not entirely fanciful: in 1619 a number of local women were hanged for witchcraft, one of the charges being that they procured the deaths of the infant heirs to Belvoir Castle by sorcery.

The art form which, while not unique to England is carried there to its highest form is that of church brasses. Some 10,000 of these survive – more than in the rest of Europe put together. Cheaper to produce than a stone sculpture, they represent a much wider social range, they also allow a flexibility of design so great that, not only is costume represented down to the smallest detail, but even early brasses can be taken as genuine portraits, providing one of our major pictorial sources of history. The oldest surviving brass in England is that of Sir John Aubernoun in Stoke d'Abernon church in Surrey along with others of his family. Sir John died in 1277 and it is uncertain whether the brass was executed at the time of his death or some years afterwards, but it is one of the finest of its kind, both in its meticulous

The Wilcote monument, North Leigh church, Oxfordshire.

*Close-up of a brass, the funerary art in which the English excelled.
A small dog lies at the foot of his master on this example in
St Peter and St Paul, Northleach, Gloucestershire.*

detail and its preservation: the shield still retains its original blue enamel. One receives a vivid impression that these portrayals were intended less as a gesture of piety, than to show off the wealth of the families which commissioned them. The brass of the wool merchant John Browne and his wife Margery in All Saints, Stamford, Lincoln-shire, seems more like a fashion plate than a *memento mori*. Not only is Mrs Browne dressed in the elaborate height of fashion but con-spicuous on John Browne is the immense purse at his girdle, as though defying the injunction 'You can't take it with you'. Brasses benefited from the Gothic revival of the nineteenth century, usually featuring high ecclesiastics, so that we have a continuous history spanning some seven centuries.

The biggest single change which a medieval parishioner would notice on returning to his church in the twentieth century would be the extraordinary clutter of pews. Even as late as 1820 William Cobbett, that sturdy defender of the traditional, was inveighing against the use of pews in churches:

'Those who built these noble buildings did not dream of disfig-uring the inside with large and deep boxes made of deal boards.

A Brass of Sir Robert de Septvans (d. 1306) in St Mary's Chartham, Kent. He is wearing a mail shirt with linen surcoat over it. Brasses, with their detailed designs, are an invaluable source of information on period costume.

Box pews in St Mary's, Whitby, North Yorkshire.
'Egad, but they worship God at their ease here' was the comment of a
French visitor, according to William Cobbett.

> This lazy lolling in pews we owe to the Reformation. A place
> filled with benches and boxes looks like an eating or drinking
> place, but certainly not a place of worship. A Frenchman went to
> church along with me one Sunday. He had never been in a
> Protestant place before. Upon looking round him and seeing
> everybody comfortably seated he exclaimed 'Pardi! on sert Dieu
> bien a son aise ici!'. That is 'Egad! They serve God very much at
> their ease here!'

Until the fourteenth century, the only seats occasionally provided in
a church would be stone benches at the base of pillars as in Moulton,
Lincolnshire or, more frequently, along the walls as at Rickinghall in
Suffolk. These were intended only for the old or disabled – hence the
phrase 'the weakest going to the wall'. Solid wooden benches began
to appear in the church in the fourteenth century and over the next
hundred years had become a general feature. But as Cobbett sur-
mised, it was the Reformation which gave the impetus to the provi-

sion of pews, particularly the boxed pew, in which, protected from draughts and reasonably comfortable, the congregation would hear out sermons lasting one, two or even three hours. Inevitably, the pew became a reflection of class, with the local grand family creating their own private space complete with sofa, table and even a fireplace where they could be served refreshments by their own servants should the sermon prove unduly long. In St Lawrence, Little Stanmore, Middlesex, the family pew of the dukes of Chandos has its own painted ceiling: the Kederminster pew in Langley Marish, Buckinghamshire, has latticework screens to provide greater privacy for the family and even boasted a small library.

The same factor which encouraged the spread of pews was responsible for the development of pulpits. They too date back to the fourteenth century – there are over 150 medieval pulpits in England – and some of the early ones are supreme works of art. Trull church in Somerset has a fifteenth century wooden pulpit with figures of the Doctors of the Church carved in splendid high relief, while Burnham Norton's in Norfolk, also of wood, still has its original painted panelling of around 1475. In the eighteenth century, the relatively modest medieval structure (usually hexagonal in shape) developed into the monstrous 'three decker'. The lower 'deck' was the place for the clerk of the parish whose job, during the service, was to lead the responses: immediately above him was the desk whence the parson read the service itself, while the upper deck was the place from which he launched his sermon at the heads of the congregation below.

The wooden lectern at St Mary's, Ottery St Mary, Devon.

Unlike the pulpit, the lectern survived the Reformation largely unchanged in form: from the beginning, the favoured shape was that of the eagle of St John, with wings outspread to hold the Gospel. Originally it was place in the chancel, but after the Reformation it was moved into the nave. The oldest surviving lectern is that in Ottery St Mary, Devon. Carved in wood and taking the well-known form of an eagle on an orb, it was given to the church by Bishop Grandison of Exeter in the fourteenth century.

Almost until our own time, the church embodied and sanctified the whole concept of social hierarchy even in death. As late as 1793 a grave by the door of the parish church of Kingsbridge in Devon, carried the mocking epitaph:

> 'Here lie I at the chancel door
> Here I lie because I'm poor
> The further in, the more you pay
> Here I lie as warm as they.'

The 'further in' of course meant as near as possible to the altar, the favoured place for a grave or chantry. Only one other place equalled or, possibly, even surpassed the altar as a guarantee to heaven, and that was adjacent to the shrine if the church was fortunate enough to possess one. It is difficult to say why the relics of a particular person were believed to possess certain sovereign virtues – especially, the ability to cure physical illnesses – and thereby became a focal point for pilgrimages. (The oddest of all these transformations are the remains of the homosexual king, Edward II, murdered by his wife's lover, which unaccountably became cult object in Gloucester cathedral). The only church which today possesses the bones of its patron saint is the little church of Whitchurch Canonicorum in Dorset, and it may be this sense of long continuity which turned the saint's tomb into a shrine. Although the person is referred to as 'St Wite' the true name and even the sex of the saint is uncertain. It was long believed the 'Wite' was a Saxon monk who, travelling through Germany, was murdered by pagan Saxons and his bones brought back home. When in 1900 the shrine was opened for repairs, a leaden box was discovered with a Latin inscription identifying the bones within as indeed being those of a 'St Wite'. The bones however were those of a woman. If she were indeed the true occupant of the shrine she may have been a Celtic princess whose name passed through a bewildering number of translations from 'Wite', a purely personal name, to the concept of colour – 'Blanche' and 'Candida' eventually giving a name to the locality. The shrine itself survives intact. Built in the thirteenth century, at least seven hundred years after the supposed lifetime of the saint, it has three distinct oval openings into which the afflicted could thrust arms or legs in search of relief. St Wystan, in Repton, Derbyshire, is another church where the last resting place of the patronal saint survives, though the actual remains of St Wystan have long since vanished. The survival, and discovery of this Saxon crypt were both accidental. In 1779 a grave digger at work in the chancel of the ancient church actually fell through the floor, only to find himself in a crypt that had been bricked up centuries before. Originally, it had been a mausoleum for the royal Saxon house of Mercia. Wystan, heir to the throne, was murdered by his godfather in 850 and was buried here. Again, we have no real indication as to why the remains of this seemingly commonplace young man should be deemed to have supernatural powers, but there is strong architectural evidence that this was the case. The entrance to the crypt today is down through steps that have evidently been cut through the walls of the mausoleum after the burial of Wystan. The worn condition of these steps are mute but eloquent testimony to the attractive power of the shrine before it was first forgotten and then bricked over.

CHAPTER VI

THE SOCIAL FABRIC

On a summer's evening 'after even-song' in the year 1451, Agnes Paston, Lady of the manor of the village of Paston in Norfolk, was seated in one of the enclosed wooden pews (which still remain in the church):

'Agnes Ball came to me and bade me good even, and Clement Spicer with her. And I asked him what he would. And he asked me why I had stopped the king's way and I said to him I had stopped no way but my own. And all that time Waryn Herman leaned over the partition and listened to what we said and said that the change was a rewly change, for the village was undo thereby and is the worse by £100. And I told him it was no courtesy to meddle in the matter, but if he were called to council'.

Still arguing heatedly, the four walked out of the church, parting at the disputed boundary. Agnes Paston hastened home to sum up the argument in a letter to her son John, a lawyer in London – and incidentally provide for posterity a sudden vivid illustration of the social role of the church as a place where people met – not as social equals, certainly, but on equal grounds.

Viewed from the twentieth century, with its plethora of distractions: its television and telephones, its newspapers, transport, radios, its vast public buildings ever increasing in size and number, viewed from this cluttered standpoint it is exceedingly difficult to grasp the social importance of the parish church before the Industrial Revolution changed the shape of our society. In any village and in most towns it was the biggest single building. Usually, it was the only public building, the only covered area where villagers or towns-folk could meet as of right. The churchyard not only contained visible evidence of the generations that had gone before – evidence banished today to vast anonymous suburban cemeteries – but was frequently a commercial centre of considerable importance, the spontaneous conversations and contacts taking place as the congregation left after a service, developing into more formalized relationships.

In the main, posterity is dependent upon such chance observations as that of Dame Agnes to get an insight into the social life of the church. In 1834, however, there was published a work which did this on a systematic basis, bringing to sudden, vivid life the workaday world of a country church. The church of St Peter in the small Shropshire village of Myddle has little to distinguish it. The austere Pevsner dismisses it in eight tight-lipped lines . . . 'rebuilt 1744: thoroughly gothicized in 1837-58 and 1877 . . . E. window commemorates somebody who died in 1847' and so on. But a generation before it was rebuilt, this modest village church provided the stage for a remarkable – indeed unique exercise in local history – nothing less than the attempt to identify the ghosts of those who sat in the pews. The author was a certain Richard Gough, born in the village in 1636, who describes himself simply as a 'yeoman'. But he was a well

Tithe barn at Paston in Norfolk.

educated yeoman, infected with the prevailing passion for antiquities. He had already produced a worthy, but dull work on the 'antiquityes' of Myddle and was 66 years old when, looking at the massed pews in the parish church he realized that they provided both a clue to the village's history and a skeleton upon which to hang that history.

In the manner of his time. Gough provided a lengthy, clumsy, but comprehensive title for his book which adequately sums up his theme *'Observations concerning the Seates in Myddle and the familyes to which they belong'*. Why did he chose such an apparently limiting subject as church pews? He defines his reason succinctly:

> 'A pew is a certain place in church incompassed with wainscott or some other thing for several persons to sit in together. A peiw may belong wholly to one family or it may belong to two or three familieys or more.' ... Then he thrusts home his point ... ' A peiw or seat does not beelong to a person or to land, butt to an house, therefore if a man renmove from an house to dwell in another, he shall not retain the seat belonging to the first house.'

Bearing that basic, unalterable principle in mind, Gough therefore set about identifying the occupants of each of the pews in Myddle church, partly using documentation, partly drawing on personal and folk memory.

Of the church itself he is as dismissive as Pevsner 250 years later:

From Gough's History of Myddle. *Was this an attempt at a self-portrait?*

St Mary the Virgin, Ottery St Mary, Devon.
Mostly rebuilt in the early fourteenth century with
magnificent stone vaulting.

Built near the earthworks of a Norman castle, the fourteenth century tower is separate from the main church of St Bartholomew, Richard's Castle, Hereford & Worcester.

Holy Trinity, Stratford-upon-Avon, Warwickshire. Shakespeare's tomb lies in front of the high altar.

'As to the time when, and by whom, the church was built, these things are long since buried in the depth of antiquity that it is impossible to make any other discovery of them'.

He did remember the rebuilding of the steeple because it was the cause of a row between the rector and the villagers. The old steeple was ruinous and the rector offered to have it rebuilt, from the foundations up to his own height at his own expense if the villagers would complete the work. They declined. The rector abandoned the idea in dudgeon and when the steeple eventually fell the villagers were obliged to have it built entirely at their expense. The mason was a certain John Dod 'I have heard that he had for his wages £5 a yard', and that was all that was of interest about the physical building.

The village of Myddle is not only small – even today the population is only about 1,000 – but also scattered. The church therefore played an unusually important role as a social centre. What comes out very clearly in Gough's meticulous work is how society was both stratified and ossified. Gough himself says, specifically in regard to a contro-versy that had arisen over who should sit where 'it was held a thing unseemly and undecent that a companye of young boyes, and of persons that paid no leawans (pew charges) should sit above those of the best of the Parish'. Even the physical structure of the pews showed class differences:

'The Thirteenth (pew) is a small seate by the South dore. It was made by Evan Jones of some waste plankes and boards that were a spare att the uniformeing of the pews.'

In the plan which Gough drew up for his readers the unfortunate Jones family, together with the Widow Groome, are shown crammed in at the very bottom of the church in front of the draughty door. Then conscientiously Gough works his way through the church, from the first pew:

'which belongs to Mr Hanmer's farm in Marton, Mr Andrew Atcherley for the lands in Marton, and Sleape Hall'

to the pew knocked up by Evan Jones. The Goughs had the right to no less than four pews, by virtue of their various properties in the village. Gough himself had a middle pew in the middle row and one gets a vivid impression of the old man quizzically regarding his neighbours, mentally noting their idiosyncrasies to enliven his genealogical notes. Thus, on the other side of the aisle from him was Thomas Jukes:

> 'a bauling, bold confident person: hee often kept company with his betters, but shewed them noe more respect than if they had been his equals or his betters. He was a great bowler, and often bowled with Sir Humphrey Lea (when) hee would make noe more account of Sir Humphrey, than if he had been an plow-boy. He would ordinarily tell him he lyed, and sometymes throw the bowle att his head, and then they parted in wrath. But within dayes Sir Humphrey would take Jukes with him to the bowles and if they did not fall out would take him home and make him drunk.'

Behind Jukes were the village villains, the Reeces:

> 'a bad husband and a pilfering thievish person and his sons were as bad as their father. They never stole any considerable goods but were night walkers and robbed oarchyards and gardens, and stole hay out of meadows.'

Two pews behind Gough sat Thomas Highway who earned the disapproval of the villagers. It was quite wrong, thought Gough that Highway, being a mere cottager and paying only 6d a year instead of the general rate of a shilling or even more, should not only have a pew, but the right of kneeling in another. Worse:

> 'He did usually give liberty to other Cottagers to sit in this seate, on condition they should pay him yearly for such liberty. This was a thing never done in this parish before.'

And so it goes on. In the 'fifth pew on the North Side of the South aisle' sat Thomas Hayward. He, poor fellow:

> 'had little quietnesse att home which caused him to frequent publick houses merely for his naturall sustenance and there meeting with companye and being generally well beeloved he stayed often too long'.... Such a way of life had only one ending ... 'He sold and consumed all his estate and was afterwards maineteined on charyte by his eldest son'.

There were the three brothers, Thomas, Andrew and John Hindley who 'were rich and allways had money beforehand'. But all three brothers died within a week of each other, the first by natural causes the other two by grief. Richard Clark, who sat near the Goughs own pews, 'hee had a smooth waye of flattering discourse, and was a perfect master in the art of dissembling.' He enlisted as a soldier for Parliament, returned some years later and married:

> 'She was very thick of heareing, butt yett she was a comely woman, and had a portion in money, which Clarke quickly spent for he was a very drunk fellowe if he could gett money to spend'.

One wonders what Dickens would have made of these rural dramas had a copy of Gough's detailed work come his way.

In its gentle, unassuming way, the *History of Myddle* unequivocally demonstrates how the parish church formed the foundation of society. It is one of the ironies of history that the term 'parish' in the English language is today used either condescendingly or contemptuously. 'Parish pump politics' is a metaphor for trivial or ephemeral affairs: 'parochial' does duty for a blinkered somewhat pompous viewpoint. But no less an authority than Beatrice and Sidney Webb, in their magisterial, if bleak survey of English local government, do not simply identify the parish as the 'cradle of democracy', but unequivocally identify it as the very means whereby society governed itself before the advent of the nation state. Until the reign of the memorable Henry VIII they point out, the parish was essentially an ecclesiastic organization created for the convenience of ecclesiastics. The name itself can be traced back to the roman empire when the *parochia* was one of the means of civic administration. The marvellously adaptive primitive Church, took the *parochia* as the natural means of administration based on the mother Church of a region. It was the commissioners of Henry VIII who again transformed the parish into

> 'a machinery which, in addition, could discharge various functions of the civil power,'

and from it grew the State which we recognise today.

The principal officers of the parish were the constable, the churchwardens, the overseers of the poor, and the waywardens, most of them discharging roles which are today the responsibility of the State. The office of constable illustrates the intricate relationship between State, manor and Church. Originally he was probably a manorial officer, keeping order on behalf of the baron. As the parish grew in importance so his powers were transferred to it. Churchwardens date back to 1129 when their office was instituted by the Council of London. Their roles were essentially ecclesiastic: responsibility for the fabric of the church, for the allocation of seats within it, the day to day running of parish business, but they also had responsibility for the spiritual oversight of the priest and his curates. Involving as it did the raising and spending of large sums of money, the work of the churchwardens placed considerable power in their hands – and in the accounting for that money their records were to provide vital primary sources of history.

The overseers of the poor were responsible to the churchwardens – and, again, their role illustrates the relationship, amounting to symbiosis of State, Church and society in general. From the very first days of the Church, care of the poor was regarded as a primary duty. The alms chest was almost as important a piece of furniture as the font, and certainly equal in importance to the pulpit. Inevitably, the *ad hoc* distribution of alms became formalized into a poor rate levied on the parishioners. In theory, a rationalization, in practice it became one of the scourges and scandals of society: churchwardens saw it as a sacred duty that outsiders should not become a 'charge on the parish' and, as corollary, that the idle should not benefit. In practice, this came to mean that the indigent were either forced on to a dreary odyssey from parish to parish, or were treated so brutally that they would hesitate to apply for relief. The term 'as cold as charity' entered the language.

A curious office, which throws considerable light on the social role of the church both before and after the Reformation, is that of the dog-whipper. Ludlow's churchwarden accounts record that a certain Thomas Payver was paid 8d in 1543 for chasing dogs out of church. A medieval illustration of the priest at the altar includes a picture of this officer, his three-thonged whip held high while a dog looks somewhat apprehensively up at him. Even as late as the seventeenth century it was decreed that the altar of a church should be surrounded by railings to keep dogs away. These precautions substantiate the fact that the nave was regarded as a purely secular place. It was the chancel together with the altar that was the sacrosanct place, while the nave belonged to the people – and their dogs. It was the stray dog which attracted the attentions of Thomas Payver and his colleagues.

At the heart of this complex of laws and customs is a figure who, like the church itself, is taken for granted but, looked at objectively, proves to be a truly extraordinary member of society. The parish priest, or parson, has again and again come under attack – frequently ferocious attack – from both extremes of society. The outward forms of his role and his powers have changed again and again over the centuries but the innermost core has remained to link the twentieth century to the figure who, in the remote past, established an altar in some wild place to act as a loadstone for Christians.

There are two main classes of parish priest, the rector and the vicar, the distinction being created in the thirteenth century. In the previous centuries, when the power of monasteries was at its height, the parish church with its endowments and tithes and bequests was taken over by a monastery as a matter of course. The monastery grew richer, the church poorer, until the Lateran Council of 1215 decreed that when a monastery, as 'rector' took over a church it had to appoint a 'vicar' and ensure that he had adequate financial provision to discharge his sacred office. Even when the power of the monastery waned, the distinction continued, for the gift of the living was only too often in the hands of the local lord of the manor. Given the English system of primogeniture, where the eldest son took the entire estate, automatically dispossessing his younger brothers, there was a standing temptation to ensure that the living was passed on to the second son. The temptation was not often resisted and there gradually grew up a system where the rectorship, with its financial rewards, virtually became hereditary, a vicar being appointed to do the actual work. The vicar was usually drawn from the lower classes and while he was thus truly the representative of his peers, the ordinary working folk, his appointment substantiated the class distinction. The education of both rector and vicar was frequently pretty basic. A decree of the Archbishop of Canterbury in 1281 seems to recognize this fact, for apart from officiating at the altar, the priest's duty was simply to

> 'expound to the people in the common tongue, without any fantastic texture of subtlety, the fourteen articles of Faith, the Ten Commandments, the Seven Works of Mercy, the Seven Deadly Sins with their progeny and the Seven Sacraments of Grace'.

In other words, his spiritual office was limited to teaching by rote, the sermon with its complex and subtle arguments being left to the preaching friars who travelled from village to village, town to town.

A certain amount of land, the glebe, was assigned to the vicar or rector for his maintenance. He could either farm it directly, (and many a country priest did so personally, unconsciously strengthening the link with his parishioners) or he could rent it out. The church's main source of income, however, was the tithes and no other church measure has aroused more bitterness over so long a period than this 'freelance taxation system operated by the Church', linking grumbling twentieth century farmer with rebellious tenth century serf. The tithe was literally the exaction of the tenth part of each parishioner's income and, until the more general use of specie, the peasant had the bitterness of seeing one sheep in ten from his flock; one chicken in ten from his backyard, even, in theory one egg in ten taken by the priest. On his side, the priest had the choice of ruthlessly pressing his claim or existing on charity. Few chose the latter course, if for no other reason than that the priest was not only responsible for the physical upkeep of the chancel but often had subordinates dependent upon him. In addition, he was supposed to allocate at least a quarter of his income to alms and hospitality.

Even as late as the seventeenth century, tithes were being paid in kind. In his *History of Myddle*, Gough gives a long list of these (the tithe of wool, lambs and geese was rendered annually, pigs every fourteen days) and notes the exceptions. At Easter the rector had 1d for every milch cow, 4d for every colt, 1d for every house with a fireplace. He also collected fees for certain priestly roles. Christenings were free but he could charge between 2s 6d and 5s for weddings. Burial in the churchyard without a coffin was 6d, with a coffin 1s – fees

Tombstones at Painswick, Gloucestershire. Some of the ninety-nine yews that embellish the churchyard are seen in the background.

which were doubled for burial actually in the church. But Gough also records a rector of Myddle who exercised his 'right to tithes' in an enchanting manner: he chose one child – a girl – from a family of ten of a poor parishioner, brought her up in his own household and eventually married her off with a handsome dowry.

On an Easter evening in 1870 the Reverend Francis Kilvert, curate of Clyro church, in Powys passed through the churchyard. It was a soft April evening, he recorded, and the churchyard was rapidly filling up with people carrying flowers.

> 'The customary beautiful Easter Eve Idyll had fairly begun and people kept arriving from all parts with flowers to dress the graves. Children were coming from the town and from neighbouring villages with baskets of flowers and knives to cut holes in the turf. The roads were lively with people coming and going and the churchyard a busy scene with women and children and a few men moving about among the tombstones and kneeling down beside the green mounds flowering the graves. More and more people kept coming into the churchyard as they finished their day's work. The sun went down in glory behind the dingle, but still the work of love went on through the twilight and into the dusk until the moon rose full and splendid. The figures continued to move about among the graves and to bend over the green mounds in the calm clear moonlight and warm air of the balmy evening'.

Kilvert's account must provide one of the last glimpses of the churchyard not simply as a cemetery, a place of horror, but as an extension of the community's social fabric, an inheritance from the distant past when the *ciric*, the 'holy ground', probably preceded the church itself. Traditionally, burials were on the south side of the church leaving the north side free for secular activities. These could include anything from serving as a children's playground, to the site for a fair, or the place where the town's merchants could foregather. In the burial area, individual tombstones were a rarity until the Reformation. The family who could afford a monument, could afford a place in the church itself: lesser people made do with the communal cross that signified the ground as holy for a permanent memorial, while the site of the grave itself would be marked with a simple wooden cross. But from about 1700 onwards, churchyard memorials appear in ever increasing numbers and variations of design. The eighteenth century is the great period for them, and outstanding in this outstanding period is the churchyard of Painswick in the Cotswolds. The churchyard is embellished with exactly 99 great yew trees, all carefully clipped (legend has it that the Devil invariably moves away the hundredth if any attempt is made to plant one). Among these handsome, sombre plants stand great chest tombs. Their number and quality reflects the fact that this delightful little town was a prosperous place not only for the wool that made the Cotswolds wealthy, but also the great quarries. It is the presence of these quarries which account for the homogeneity and number of the memorials while the detailed carving upon them is the work of an outstanding local family of masons.

Until the late nineteenth century churchyard memorials, like the church itself, were created out of local materials. Some of the most exquisite are those in slate-producing areas, the flexibility of the medium allowing the most intricate designs and lengthy epitaphs. There is a wealth of symbolism, curiously of a different order from the older symbolism in the church itself. Doves and olive branches signify 'peace', eternity is a snake that swallows itself, while 'time' is the elegant hour-glass, frequently with wings. 'Death' comes in many forms: as the traditional skeleton, frequently armed with an arrow or spear; as an urn or sarcophagus; as plucked and broken flowers, shattered pillars or a fallen tree. Some tombstones have remarkably elaborate scenes. Thomas Wood, a mason of Bingham in Nottinghamshire, produced detailed pastoral scenes of the surrounding countryside. More usual are details of Biblical subjects. The eighteenth and early nineteenth centuries are also the great period for lengthy epitaphs: some with a touch of wry humour such as the epitaph to a coachman in Hungerford churchyard in Berkshire:

'Passengers of every age I safely drove from stage to stage till death came by in a hearse unseen and stopped the course of my machine'.

Thomas Scaife, an 'engineer' on the Birmingham and Gloucester Railway who was killed when the boiler of his locomotive exploded, not only has an enchanting engraving of the locomotive on his tombstone but a lengthy poem beginning:

'My engine now is cold and still no water does my boiler fill'. . .

. . likening his death to that of a locomotive that has ceased working.

Undoubtedly the most famous of all epitaphs is that which appears on Shakespeare's tomb in Stratford-upon-Avon, Warwickshire, with its mixture of plea and warning not to disturb his bones. Its meaning

Monuments on the north side of the chancel,
Stratford-upon-Avon, Warwickshire.

has remained a puzzle to generations of scholars but the probability is that Shakespeare did not want his remains to finish up in the charnel house that was immediately adjacent to the church. A simple calculation will show that the number of inhumations in an ancient churchyard in even a small village must, over the centuries, run into many hundred, while inhumations in town churchyards, will number thousands. The surface of the churchyard in St John Maddermarket in Norwich is about 5 feet above the level of the surrounding ground, graphic – and by no means unusual – indication of the practice of stacking one burial above another. In course of time, each new burial must be at the expense of its predecessors, disturbing the remains of the previous occupants and, in addition, every enlargement or major alteration to the church would unearth more remains. At an early period, therefore, it became customary to store them in a charnel house or 'bonehole', sometimes attached to the church as at Stratford, but more usually under it in the form of a crypt. The crypt at Hythe church in Kent has a vast collection of remains, the skulls neatly arranged on shelves, rather unnervingly resembling merchandise on display in a shop.

Wordsworth's grave in the churchyard at Grasmere, Westmorland.

The fifteenth century oak chest at Lower Peover Church, Cheshire.
The chest has been used for centuries to keep records.

Hythe church also possesses an enormous iron chest which was reputedly salvaged from an Armada galleon. It was evidently intended to hold some impressive treasure for there are no less than eleven bolts, operated by the central lock, which fly back with a tremendous crash when the key is turned. The parish chest was, for centuries, truly the treasure chest of the community and while it may not have held negotiable treasures of gold and silver, it held something of even greater importance – the community's memory in the form of the parish register. Until the first census of 1801, the parish register provides us with our only reasonably accurate demographic view of the preceding 350 years. It was Elizabeth I, who in 1538, decreed that every parish church should maintain a register listing baptisms, marriages and burials. Twenty years later, a further decree went out that all registers should be copied into parchment books for their better preservation. One can almost hear the sigh of resignation as all over the country parish clerks or parsons took down the crumbling register of the past two decades and painstakingly copied their information. It is for this reason many registers show the same handwriting over what appears to be twenty years and more – not because the parsons of those parishes enjoyed unusual longevity, but because they had conscientiously obeyed the decree. For the first time, it is possible to get a true, if tantalisingly disjointed picture of the community's vital statistics. Burials soar in time of plague: there is an increase in marriages in times of greater prosperity for people marry at a younger age. Baptisms, too, reflect outside causes. Thus in Plymouth only 123 baptisms were recorded in 1589. The reason? Most of the men of Plymouth were at sea during the previous tremendous year of the Armada. Things returned to normal the following years with 181 baptisms in 1589 and 239 in 1591 – a remarkably similar pattern to that in the year or so immediately after World War II.

There are other treasures within the parish chest: the churchwarden's accounts; deeds of gifts for charities; rate books for overseers of the poor. Richard Gough provides a lively account of the vicissitudes of these records. He wanted to copy the orders made at a parish meeting in 1658 but had difficulty in tracking them down:

'These Orders were written in the Parish booke of accompts and the leafe was torn out, which leafe I have at last got the custody of and doe intend to leave it in [my] book to be kept in the Parish Chest. It is said that two leaves were torne out of the [Parish] booke, and I did for some time beleive it, but now I beleive I was mistaken. I since find it was a coppy of this leafe'.

It is upon the labours of such devoted men as Richard Gough that so much of our history is erected.

'The inhabitants of this parish may truly and with comfort say that they have, within their own limits, all those good things (wine and oil excepted) which Jesus the wise son of Sirach reckons the chief and principal things for the whole Use of man's life: viz. water, salt, iron, fire and bread: flour and wheat: honey, milk and oil and clothing and an house to cover shame. In a word, they freely enjoyed the four elements – Fire, Air, Water and earth and have each of them very good'.

So, in the early eighteenth century the local antiquary wrote of his parish of Warton in north Lancashire. Over the next century, that sense of being virtually a self-contained universe was to break down under the unprecedented changes of the Industrial Revolution. But the *idea* of the parish as a community continued and continues. It was expressed most clearly in the ceremony known as the 'Beating of the

Bounds' whereby the limits of the parish were re-established and imprinted, in particular, upon the rising generation. Some 50 years after the Lancashire writer extolled his little universe, in Norfolk Parson Woodforde was recording one such occasion of the beating of the bounds. It was a May morning in the year 1780.

'About half past 9 o'clock this morning my Squire called on me. And I took my mare and went with him to the Hart where most of the Parish were assembled to go the Bounds of the Parish and at 10 we all set off about 30 in number'.

As on most social occasions connected with Parson Woodforde, it was a convivial as well as a legal event, with a number of breaks at which the company took liquor 'and which I paid, being usual for the Rector'. The squire, Mr Press Custance, was with them, as well as a number of old men who drew on their memories to determine the route, and received the very large sum of half a guinea apiece from Mr Custance. At various points along the route the bounds were marked by the simple means of slashing a conspicuously place tree; 'Where there were no trees to mark, Holes were made and stones cast in'.

In many a country district, some of the landmarks chosen to mark the bounds were an invitation to later litigation. In Surrey in 1741 one such itinerary reads:

'An olde elm tree in the hedge of Mrs ede's garden . . . a pollard tree next the London road: a cross cut in an elm board.'

In the open fields compass directions were given in a manner which would have taxed the ability of a mariner:

'west of Mr Steer's field, then turn a circular corner north west then walk eastward on the north side of the south hedge . . . '

In the nature of things many of the landmarks would decay in time or be removed – not always innocently – so that the laborious task of beating the bounds was a very real necessity.

Today, the ceremony of beating the bounds is usually a self-conscious revival, part of our obsession with re-creating the past. But in the very heart of London, in the City itself, there takes place every three years a variation of the ceremony which, though executed as a lighthearted piece of antiquarianism, nevertheless has a curious cutting edge to it. For some 700 years the parish church of All Hallows by the Tower has lived in a somewhat prickly relationship with its mighty neighbour, the Tower of London. The parish bounds of the church coincide with the bounds of the City of London – and is the demarcation point between the City and the Tower Liberties, the Liberties being under the control of the Crown. The church beats its bounds every year, to the delight of press photographers, for one of the bounds passes down the centre of the Thames, and it is customary to hold a choirboy upside down on a barge while he beats the water with a willow wand. Every three years, however, the Tower, too, beats its bounds and then what is known as a 'confrontation' takes place. It is lighthearted enough, although in the past such confrontations frequently led to bloodshed. But the spectator watching the choirboys of the church capering up and down, making disrespectful gestures at their opposite numbers from the Tower – gestures not infrequently echoed by their sober elders – is made aware of the realities of the territorial imperative.

CHAPTER VII

THE WORLD TURNED UPSIDE DOWN

For over 1,000 years Western Europe had been shaped and directed by a single Christian ethos. There might be regional variations arising out of racial characteristics, but all subscribed to a common concept, followed a common liturgy, had a common Faith. Even when there were basic changes in that Faith, basic changes in the liturgy, these changes spread out from the centre in a slow wave that eventually reached to all parts of the periphery.

In the sixteenth century, within a generation, this apparent homogeny shattered, the fragments taking on a life of their own, and in their turn, budding off new developments. In England, the vast changes centred round the portly figure of Henry VIII although Henry was as much symptom as cause. It did so happen that he wanted, desperately wanted, something which the Bishop of Rome refused to let him have – a divorce from Katharine of Aragon. But even if he had been the most chaste husband of Queen Katharine and the most obedient of the sons of Pope Clement, changes would have come about, for the ferment of the Renaissance was working throughout Europe.

Initially, the outward signs of change in England were small enough. In 1534 the Act of Supremacy turned the King of England into 'Supreme Head of the Church of England' but Henry himself remained a good Catholic. There is, indeed, no little irony in the fact that the proud title of Defender of the faith (whose abbreviated Latin version *Fid. Def*. appeared on the coins of Britain until well into the twentieth century) was bestowed upon Henry by a grateful pope in response to Henry's own attack on the heretic, Martin Luther. The services in the churches of England went on in their immemorial way, with only one difference – they were in English. Also now deposited on public view in each church, the Bible – in English. There is, again, a profound irony in that just 14 years before the Great Bible was published, William Tyndale was burned at the stake for heresies which included translating the Bible into the vernacular. The title-page of this superb production unequivocally stated the new theological position: the throned king is shown receiving the Word of God direct from God, and handing it to the bishops who in turn, hand it down to the laity. The Royal Arms, too, began to appear in churches. But the first physical changes to the ancient religion was the Dissolution of the Monasteries – an act of destruction which, paradoxically, immensely increased the stock of parish churches.

The speed with which the 1,000 year old monastic system fell apart was astonishing: the Act was passed in 1536 and by 1540 virtually all the 500 or so abbeys, monasteries and convents had disappeared. In many cases their disappearance was literally physical. The vast abbey of Glastonbury, Somerset, bigger than the town itself, disappeared in its entirety except for the abbot's kitchen and some ruined walls. The speed of the physical destruction argues that the ordinary people of England enthusiastically backed up their king, in this matter at least. Later hindsight was to give a romantic gloss to the relationship between laity and monastery that, judging by the frequent reports of brawls between the two, was by no means the norm. Europe's debt to the monastery was enormous. Not only did it provide the means of education, but it also provided a buffer – a safety net – for the weak and helpless in society which saw no particular reason to legislate for the vulnerable. It also brought civilization to remote and barbaric districts. But its wealth and enormous power – the abbot answered not to the local, territorial bishop, but to the distant Bishop of Rome – inevitably brought corruption and a dangerous arrogance.

The tendency of monasteries to take over parish churches – and with it parish incomes – was a widespread source of irritation. In Surrey, 16 churches and their parishes – a third of those in the county – had been taken over by the monasteries; St Mary's Abbey in York held 14 churches; and in Yorkshire as a whole – one of the major concentrations of monasteries – 392 churches out of the 622 in the county were the property of monasteries. Their attitude towards layfolk did little to create harmony. In Abingdon, Berkshire, the town cemetery lay within the precincts of the abbey. In 1391 the monks, irritated by the 'intrusion of mourners' disturbing their offices, closed the cemetery. The townsfolk created a burial ground adjacent to their parish church – but the monastery continued to demand fees associated with burial and which now went into the parish chest. Rome intervened: the parishioners were obliged to close their cemetery and move their dead back into the abbey grounds, paying the heavy cost of removal as well as again paying burial dues to the monastery.

St Mary and St Hardulph, Breedon-on-the Hill, Leicestershire,
contains an important series of Saxon sculptures.

St Laurence, Bradford-on-Avon, Wiltshire.
Perhaps the most perfect survival of a Saxon church it was
rediscovered in the nineteenth century.

St Bride's, Fleet Street, London. World War II air raids uncovered Saxon, Roman and Norman remains all now on display in the crypt.

St John the Evangelist, Wotton, Surrey.
The parish church of John Evelyn, the diarist, who is buried here.

Wymondham Abbey, Norfolk, Lincolnshire.
The dispute between monks and laity as to who owned which part of
the building is reflected by the separate towers built by each party.

A frequent source of discord was the presence of parochial altars in monastic churches. The people of Wymondham in Norfolk were obliged to use the abbey church as the parish church, but so bitter were the quarrels between monks and townsfolk, so endless the rows regarding who owned which part of the church, that the bishop intervened, decreeing that the nave and north aisle of the church belonged to the town. The townsfolk made the division concrete as well as legal, building a wall over the rood screen. Even this division did not stop the quarrels, and in the fifteenth century both parties built their own immense, bell towers, one at each end of the church and totally different from each other in design.

The wealth of the greater monasteries – in particular those of popular shrines such as Becket's at Canterbury, Kent, and Swithin's in Winchester, Hampshire – automatically found its way into the Royal Exchequer. The buildings themselves were sold for a song, usually to the king's friends, and were either demolished for the sake of their materials, or transformed into a nobleman's home: the

(Left) St Bartholomew, Smithfield, London: the church-yard occupies what was the nave, demolished after the Reformation. The present entrance to the church is actually through the west side of the crossing.

number of stately homes, such as Woburn Abbey, which include the title 'prior' or 'abbey' in their name is significant. But many towns, too, were able to save the monastic church by claiming that it had always been their parish church – but they paid for the privilege. Thus the Crown sold the superb abbey church at Tewkesbury, Gloucestershire, to the town for the substantial sum of £453. There are over 80 of these 'collegiate' or monastic churches in England. Many consist simply of the nave, or the chancel with later additions. But many such churches have survived in their entirety, such as the magnificent abbey churches at Sherborne in Dorset and Romsey in Hampshire. The distinguishing mark of these churches is their enormous size in relation to the often minute towns (the remains of Malmesbury Abbey in Wiltshire, for example, tower above a town of around 3,000 people) and their extraordinary truncated appearance. The visitor opens a door, or goes through an arch, expecting to enter another part of the church – and is outside. One of the most dramatic of these survivals is that of St Bartholomew in London.

Founded in 1123 it survived Henry VIII's onslaught, the fury of the Puritan iconoclasts, the Great Fire of London and the massive air raids of World Ward II. The medieval gatehouse leads not into the nave, as one would expect (in the thirteenth century it was the south entrance) but into a small churchyard. On the right-hand side however one can see remains of the south aisle wall. The entrance into the church itself is through what used to be the south side of the crossing but the whole was built on so vast a scale that the remains seem a

*St Bartholomew, Smithfield, London: the church was built on
such a vast scale that even though the nave was demolished
the remainder seems complete.*

complete church. Wymondham Church in Norfolk is another such survival with the two extraordinary towers soaring up to provide dramatic testimony of the conflicts between monks and laity.

The first, physical, part of the church to endure change as a result of the new dispensation was the chantry. Here, again, the motive was partly greed to get at the valuable endowments, but partly a desire to reform 'superstitious practices'. As early as 1519, seven years before the onslaught on monasteries, Parliament passed an Act forbidding any priest to accept a chantry appointment after Michaelmas that year. In theory, their endowments survived even the Act of Dissolution of the Monasteries. It was not until 1545, five years after the last monastery had passed into oblivion, that an Act formally transferred their property to the Royal Exchequer 'for good and godly uses' – the pious king Henry VIII being the arbiter of what constituted a good and godly use. It was a curious oversight on the part of that acquisitive monarch, for the cannier of the great families whose ancestors had provided the endowment of the chantries had had nearly ten years to see which way the wind was blowing, and had taken care that the endowments found their way into their own coffers.

Henry VIII died in 1547: his sickly adolescent son Edward VI came to the throne, inaugurating one of the most dizzying, most confusing periods in English history. For a little over 100 years the pendulum swung violently to and fro, now Catholic, now Protestant, now monarchist, now parliamentarian. A hundred years during which the usually tolerant English countenanced the burning alive of their compatriots for minute divergencies of religious opinion, beheaded their anointed king, and saw finally, the notion of Christian unity shatter into scores of fragments.

It was the chantries which felt the first of the blows. Henry had not had time to activate his Act before he died, but within a few weeks of his death his son's 'advisers' made good the oversight. Their Act of 1547 authorized wholesale plunder:

'Our Sovereign Lord the King shall have and enjoy all such goods, chattels, jewels, plates, ornaments and other moveables as were or be the common goods of every such college, chantry, free chapel or stipendiary priest, belonging or annexed to the furniture or services of the several foundations'.

Not only the 'superstitious' chantries were included in this but also the almshouses attached to the churches, which had brought succour to thousands of indigent poor. Over 100 of these went, together with more than 2,000 guilds and chantries. The anchorites, too, were suppressed, ending a tradition that went back to the earliest days of the Christian Church. All this was done in the name of the boy king. In fact this, the last great plundering of the churches of England, was largely a freelance operation – most of the loot finding its way into the pockets of private citizens. In an operation rather reminiscent of the plunder of central America by the Spaniards, the churches of England were stripped of treasures that had been accumulating for over five centuries in a little over a decade. In a few cases, devoted churchwardens were able to anticipate the so-called 'commissioners' to the benefit of their own people: the wardens of St Lawrence in Reading sold the remains of their church plate for £47. 18s on behalf of the parish; those of Holy Trinity in Coventry sold nine copes of valuable velvet for a total of £126.10s. But few parishes benefited in this manner. Long Melford in Suffolk lost 16 valuable copes, 38 altar cloths, altar vessels of precious metals coming to the incredible total of 900 ounces, as well as a variety of personal ornaments such as rings, girdles, and buckles. Warrington in Northamptonshire, lost the very bells in the belfry, as well as altar vessels of precious metals, and vestments adorned with gems.

That was only the beginning. Hard on the heels of open plunder came the directives for the onslaught on the church itself. The edict went out that everything 'vain and superstitious' should forthwith be destroyed or removed. Now it was that the great rood, with its frequently life-sized figures of Christ, the Madonna, and St John, its exquisite carvings and lively paintings, was hacked down and burnt. The actual shrines, having been plundered of their valuable ornaments, were smashed, wall paintings whitewashed, statues defaced, the very brass on tombs ripped out.

The separation of priest from laity was particularly offensive to the reformers. In 1551 the Bishop of Gloucester instructed the clergy to

'remove all partitions within your churches, whereat any mass hath been said and so to make the church without any closure and separation between ministers and people'.

Again, a concept that had endured since the very earliest days, the concept of a sacred area, a 'holy of holies', was destroyed. The high altar itself came in for furious attack: the very idea of an 'altar' with its connotations of sacrifice was repugnant. In its place came the 'communion table' – a plain construction of wood, and this was to be brought into the nave. The massive stone slab of the altar was dragged out of the chancel and other side altars dismantled: in St Stephen's Walbrook it took five labourers working for three days to remove all the altars. Mostly they were sold for a few pence, sometimes to be broken up, sometimes to be used as paving slabs. A number of these, distinguished by the five consecration crosses, survive on the floor of churches, or in churchyards, round the country. At Cobham in Kent, the original slab of the high altar now forms part of the chancel paving, while two such slabs lie in the churchyard at Hartland in Devon. The 'superstitious' images having been whitewashed over (and so, ironically, preserved for posterity), texts taken from Holy Scripture were inscribed in their place and stained glass windows wither their 'blasphemous' images of Christ and the Apostles were smashed as a matter of course.

The iconoclasts did not have it all their own way. The beautiful little church of St Margaret's, hard by Westminster Abbey, escaped total destruction only because an angry mob chased the workers away. The incident displays, in the clearest possible form, the deep cynicism and opportunism that was at work simultaneously with the passionate desire for reform. The Duke of Somerset, the so-called Protector, was engaged in building his immense new palace on the Strand, and St Margaret's provided a useful source of stone. The workmen had actually erected their scaffolding and begun to demolish it when the mob threatened their lives. Somerset's action was, admittedly, extreme, and few churches faced quite such a threat, but neither did the parishioners of most make any particular attempt to protect the treasures heaped up by their forefathers. By the time the sickly Edward VI had ended his brief life, and his half-sister Mary had come to the throne, the work of destruction and desecration was far advanced.

Now the pendulum began to swing the other way, as Mary, as fanatical in her way as any Puritan, sought to return the Church to the position it had occupied before the Reformation. Elaborate ceremonies with gorgeously robed priests, incense, acolytes and all the trappings of the Church of Rome took the place of austere sermonising. The communion table was banished, the altar replaced in the chancel, the mystic qualities of the priest enhanced by physical separation from the laity. It is possible that, if Mary had been content to re-establish the Church as had been intended by her terrifying father – a fully Catholic but autonomous Church no longer under the control of Rome – the people of England might well have acquiesced. But she wanted more than that: she wanted a return to the *status quo ante*, even to the extent of linking herself indissolubly with England's most formidable enemy, Philip of Spain. By the time she died, all she had succeeded in doing was persuading the English that patriotism and Protestantism were synonymous and that only traitors embraced the ancient religion of Europe.

The sixteenth century saw the efflorescence of a superb architecture in England – but it was almost entirely a civic and domestic architecture, for church building had come to an abrupt halt. However, though the churches might stand gaunt and bare compared with what they had been half a century before, the work of destruction ceased. Elizabeth was as robust a Protestant as her half-sister Mary had been a devout Catholic, not hesitating to let her displeasure at Romish practices be known. 'Away with those torches for we see very well', she shouted, when the Abbot of Westminster and his chapter came to meet her in full canonicals. But she was a daughter of her time: the time was the dawning of the Renaissance in England, and during her reign the violent swings of the religious pendulum seemed to have come to a civilized rest. In 1560 she ordered that 'the tables of the Commandments be comely set or hung up in the east end of the chancel', and parishioners were ordered to attend church under penalties. But it seemed as though the almost lunatic fanaticism of the years immediately following the death of Henry VIII was at an end.

It came back, with renewed force, within a generation of Elizabeth's own death in 1603, as the Puritans of Cromwellian England finished what their brethren had commenced in the reign of Edward VI. But before it returned there was a brief interlude in which an entirely new architectural form was born.

Inigo Jones is probably the first person in England who can be positively identified as an 'architect' – that is, some one who has studied a variety of architectural forms, foresees the technical problems, and brings all aspects of the art together to form a predetermined, unified whole. Yet this was only one aspect of a remarkable man. He began his career as a species of stage designer, creating the fashionable masques for the court of James I. Born in 1573 he was not only in the mainstream of Renaissance thought, but had gone to the fountain head itself – twice he had visited Italy. His first visit was in order to study painting, but on his second visit, in 1613, he made a specific study of the new 'classical' architecture, inspired by Palladio, which was blossoming throughout the country. On his return to England he became Surveyor of the King's Works – in effect, the Royal Architect – and in that capacity designed the first truly classical house in England, the Queen's House at Greenwich, and the first place of worship in the classical style – the Queen's Chapel in St James's Palace. He now added a third to that remarkable achievement – England's first classical parish church – St Paul's Covent Garden in London.

Even without Jones's contribution, Covent Garden would be a

notable innovation. True to the tradition of their Saxon forebears, the English ever preferred to adapt, adjust and modify rather than plan overall. The great London landowner, the Earl of Bedford, was therefore quite literally breaking new ground when, in 1631 he proposed a major property development which would consist, not only of 'houses fit for the habitation of Gentlemen and men of ability', but also all the amenities which a gentleman would expect to find near his home. Among these amenities a Christian gentleman expected a church. The idea of a brand new church on a virgin site – the very first to be built since the Reformation – bristled with difficulties. The Earl himself was what would later be called 'low church' and would certainly have disapproved strongly if his architect dabbled with 'Romish' concepts which meant, in effect, any return to the Gothic. Yet Puritanism had not yet tightened its grip on the English church. There was still the feeling that the house of God should in some way be different from a secular building. Finally, the Earl, though a man of taste, was careful to the point of parsimony, informing his architect that the church was to be no more elaborate than a barn. Jones's reply has passed into architectural history, 'Well, then you shall have the handsomest barn in England'.

In choosing Inigo Jones as his architect, the Earl of Bedford chose perhaps the only man in England who could walk the tightrope between extravagance and austerity, who could create a building that would reflect its high purpose and yet not cause offence to the godly with unnecessary ornamentation. He achieved his aim by going back some 2,000 years and using the sacred buildings of ancient Greece as a model. But it was a model that had passed through a process of subtle changes over the centuries, first through the hands of the Romans and then yet again through the hands of the architects of the Italian Renaissance. Unlike the exuberant architecture which had flourished in Western Europe culminating in the splendid extravaganza of Gothic, Greek architecture was austere, relying for its effect on proportions. In the form that it had come to Inigo Jones, it consisted of three 'orders': Doric, plain and strong; Ionic, elegant; and Corinthian with its elaborately decorated capital. The Romans had added two more orders: the Composite, combining the elements of Ionic and Corinthian; and the Tuscan, resembling the Doric but even plainer. When these came to be used for churches in Italy, Renaissance architects recommended certain orders for certain kinds of churches: thus the relatively plain, strong Doric was to be used for churches dedicated to male saints; the Corinthian for virgins – the Madonna in particular; and the Ionic for older female saints and men of learning. The Tuscan was generally supposed to be appropriate only for

*'The handsomest barn in England': Inigo Jones's portico at
St Paul's, Covent Garden, London.*

buildings associated with castles – and prisons. It is therefore curious
that Inigo Jones chose this last style for his church. His reasons were
probably twofold: being plain, it would be cheaper to build and so suit
his patron's pocket, but being plain it would also not offend his
patron's religious belief.

Both the Earl and his architect intended that St Paul's should be the
focal point of the Covent Garden development. Over the following
centuries, as the area became ever more commercialized, so the church
lost something of its topographical importance. But the postwar
development of Covent Garden has again brought this plain, handsome church into prominence. Jones had intended that the entrance
should be, in the classical manner, through the great portico on the
east but Archbishop Laud insisted that the altar should be placed in

its now traditional position, on the east, with the entrance on the west. It irritated the architect but it has proved a fortunate decision in the light of the modern development, for the great portico now forms a natural stage for many of the social activities which characterize the area.

Inigo Jones and his parsimonious master had achieved a notable first, laying the foundations for the greatest of all English architects. But before Wren came on the scene to combine, with a genius's touch, the multiforms of architecture from the extravagant to the austere – into the single, joyous, truly English style of the Baroque, there took place one more convulsion of Puritan fanaticism, a convulsion so severe that even now we are seeking to repair its damage.

It was fortunate that Jones had chosen so austere a model for his church, for in 1641, just eight years after it was completed, in another violent swing of the pendulum, Parliament passed an Act ordering the destruction of 'all scandalous pictures' and Parliamentary Commissioners were established to ensure that the order was obeyed down to its smallest detail. The order went far beyond the destruction of religious 'pictures' alone. In the words of the seventeenth century historian, Weever:

> 'Under colour of this, their commission and in their too forward zeal, they rooted up and battered down crosses in churches and churchyards'.

In his grave and measured tones, the writer goes on to emphasize that the monuments did not even have to have a religious significance:

> 'They defaced and brake down the images of kings, princes and noble estates erected, set up or portrayed for the only memory of them to posterity and not for any religious honour.'

Foremost among these destroyers was a certain William Dowsing, and rarely indeed has a man so enthusiastically provided a rope by which posterity can hang him. He achieved this by keeping a journal, remarkable for its brusque brutality, in which he meticulously described his work. Dowsing was appointed to the deceptively respectable office of Parliamentary Visitor under the warrant of the Earl of Manchester,

> 'for demolishing the superstitious pictures, ornaments etc in the county of Suffolk',

and the depredations he records extend for only ten months, from January to October 1643, although other evidence shows that he was at work over a much longer period. His energy was astonishing: in the January and February he seems to have stopped work only on Sundays, and on one day, 6 January, he visited six localities. His raids seem to have been planned on no obvious principle apart from that of destruction. On 26 January he started at Saxmundham in the north, 'where we took up 2 superstitious inscriptions in brass', then rode southward visiting another six widely separated towns and villages on that short winter's day. Logically continuing on the next day, a Saturday, to Ufford, they had a field day:

'We brake down 30 superstitious pictures and gave direction to take down 37 more and 40 cherubim to be taken down of wood and the chancel levelled. There was a picture of Christ on the Cross and God the father above: and left 37 pictures to be taken down and 6 superstitious inscriptions in brass'.

They went on to the beautiful little market town of Woodbridge, in Suffolk. Unaccountably they spared the superb church of St Mary on that occasion, but wheeling round, Dowsing and his assistants re-traced their steps to Rushmere, nearly 20 miles to the north, where

'We brake down the picture of the 7 deadly sins and the Holy Lamb with the Cross above it and 15 other superstitious pictures.'

Sometimes it was necessary to return to a church as at Ufford, and, seeming not content with the mayhem wreaked on 27 January, they attacked again on 31 August. Apparently, the parishioners had been reluctant to take down the '7 superstitious pictures' and Dowsing now returned to do it for them. He seems, oddly enough, to have had an aesthetic sense, for at Ufford church he remarked:

'There is a glorious cover over the Font like a Pope's triple crown with a pelican on the top picking its breast, all gilded with gold.'

(Did this, one wonders, survive? The editor of the *Journal*, writing about 1786 notes that 'Several elegant drawings of this venerable remains have lately been made'). At Ufford, Dowsing and his men met with the sullen resistance of the villagers:

'We were kept out of the church above two hours and neither of the churchwardens would not (*sic*) let us have the key'.

More than once the destroyers met opposition, not simply passive as at Ufford but also an outright refusal to pay the statutory fee of 6s/8d demanded for the services provided. For, again, one detects the pragmatism behind the fanaticism: image-breaking was a job like any other and was not the labourer worthy of his hire? The churchwarden's accounts of Blythburgh in Suffolk bear a number of glum entries on the subject:

> 'Paid to master Dowson that came with the troopers to our Church about the taking down of images and brasses off stones: 6s 0d.' . . . 'Paid that day to others for taking up the brasses of Gravestones before the officer Dowson came 1s 0d.'

Presumably this last entry refers to a pre-empting on the part of the

Holy Trinity church and the Hall at Staunton Harold Leicestershire. Defying the Cromwellian strictures, Sir Robert Shirley of Staunton Harold Hall paid for the building of Holy Trinity in the traditional style.

Above the west entrance of Holy Trinity, Staunton Harold,
a plaque states: 'In the Year 1653 when all things Sacred were
throughout ye nation Either demolisht or profaned,
Sir Robert Shirley, Baronet, Founded this church'.
Shirley finished up in the Tower of London for his pains.

churchwardens – the brass being quietly sold and so denying it to the 'commissioners'. Blythburgh church bears a particularly poignant example of destruction. Unable to reach the carvings that adorn the immensely high ceiling of the church, the commissioners fired at them, peppering the serene faces of the angels with lead shot. They still clearly bear the scars.

To the victorious Puritans it must have seemed that the godly had finally and permanently triumphed with the pagan temple, not simply cleansed of idolatrous images, but the building itself stripped of its supernatural aura and reduced to the status of an ordinary structure. Admittedly, the number of churches in which Cromwell was supposed to have stabled his horses must equal the number of houses in which Elizabeth was supposed to have slept, but the buildings seem to have lost significance even for those who were supposed to be defending their cause. Royalists barricaded themselves in the church at Alton in Hampshire, fighting it out to the death: their commander, Colonel Boles, was shot down as he stood in the pulpit and the doorway and pillars of the church still bear the marks of the fusillades fired by both sides. But the triumph of the Puritans ended with the death of Cromwell. The Restoration of the monarch and with it, the restoration of the Church of England, again established the concept that aesthetic appeal did not necessarily militate against religious sincerity.

Traditional church building had not come to a complete halt during the Commonwealth but the very choice of architecture was a political, as well as a religious matter. In Leicestershire a staunch Royalist, Sir Robert Shirley, built a church in the Gothic style on his estate at Staunton Harold. The church, tucked inside its neat encircling walls on the lawn in front of the great house, today more resembles a rich man's toy, a folly to decorate a garden, than a statement of religious intent. But it was a direct challenge to Parliament. Cromwell was furious: if Sir Robert could afford to build a papistical church, he declared, Sir Robert could also afford to provide a regiment for Parliament. Sir Robert refused to do so and ended his days in the Tower of London as a consequence. But the church at Staunton Harold is a rarity. The characteristic religious building of the Commonwealth was more a akin to the Walpole Chapel in Suffolk. Built in 1647, architecturally it is entirely satisfying, the forerunner of the great Nonconformist chapels of the eighteenth century. But essentially it is a chamber for instruction and reflection, a place dedicated to reason, rather than emotion, and certainly not a 'church' as conceived by a millennium of Christian worship. A genius was needed to bridge the gap, and that genius was Christopher Wren.

Wren's influence on architecture was so enormous, the imprint he placed upon London so distinctive and widespread, that hindsight tends to regard his advent as inevitable, as though he effortlessly stepped out on a stage that was prepared for him. That this was by no means the case is well illustrated by the fact that the commissioners responsible for the rebuilding of St Paul's after the Great Fire, were initially most reluctant to countenance an entire rebuilding. Obedient to that English preference to patch up and adapt rather than build afresh, their original instructions to Wren were that the choir might perhaps be rebuilt entirely, but the rest of the ancient building should be restored. Happily, the damage it had suffered made restoration a practical impossibility, and Wren was free to create his great church from the ground upwards.

In addition to the loss of St Paul's cathedral, the great Fire of London destroyed 84 parish churches. Wren rebuilt 51 of these. He was faced with two major problems, one physical, the other theological. The physical problem was the irregular shape of the sites of the churches. Old St Paul's had been so vast, and the cathedral of the Bishop of London so important, that he had a clear site upon which to place his building. By contrast, the parish churches had been hemmed in by centuries of casual, unplanned development. Some had extended their areas, adding an aisle here, extending an apse there, others had contracted – each was quite unique in ground plan.

The theological problem was that these churches were, with the exception of Inigo Jones's Covent Garden church, the first to be built with a purely Anglican worship in mind. Christopher Wren – an intellectual, a Fellow of the Royal Society, by training a mathematician and astronomer – was entirely attuned to the new 'rational' attitude of the English Church, entirely out of sympathy with all that had gone before. After all, it was he who contemptuously labelled the ecclesiastical architecture of his forebears as 'Gothic' meaning 'barbaric'. He was quite clear as to the function of his churches. It was enough for the churches built for the Romanists, he said

'if they hear the Murmur of the Masses, and see the Elevation of the Host, but ours are fitted for Auditories'.

In the hands of a lesser man, the intention to build a church where the sermon was the main function could have resulted in a bleak box. In Wren, the architect blended with the mathematician and the astronomer to create a structure where proportion, and cool, balanced order conveyed the same sense of a sacred building as the romanticism of the 'Gothic' period.

The Age of Reason. Wren's church of
St Stephen, Walbrook, London,
designed as an auditorium rather than a theatre.

St Stephen, Walbrook is the church usually cited as Wren's supreme masterpiece among parish churches. The building is smaller than its predecessor so Wren was able to dictate the ground plan. Apart from the entrance lobby, the church is a perfect rectangle and within it one can see, in concrete form, the mathematician working out a mystic plan. Sixteen splendid Corinthian columns are so arranged to give a different vista from different angles, making the interior seem far larger than it is. The centre is dominated by a superb dome, weighing some 50 tons – the first to be built in England, and later serving as a prototype for the gigantic dome of St Paul's cathedral. The whole is flooded with light, itself symbolic of the light bestowed by reason. The 'auditory' aspect has unfortunately been reduced by the removal of the box pews. The pillars are so designed that the pews would have fitted smugly into the square bases, creating again a visual harmony – somewhat lost today by the presence of temporary looking chairs and benches.

CHAPTER VIII

LIFE IN THE RECTORY

In the twentieth century, the country rectory is a millstone around the neck of the Church Commissioners. Vast mansions designed to thrust home the social status of their incumbents, they have broken the heart of many a parson's wife or daughter struggling to maintain the monsters on inadequate incomes and an ever decreasing staff. Throughout the country, the tendency today is to sell them off, using the money raised to build a modern rectory closer to the new centre of population. A hybrid, the end product of the violent clashes of the post Reformation years, the rectory has also been the seed bed for an astonishing range of talents. Early in this century Bishop Welldon, ex-headmaster of Harrow conscientiously went through the pages of the recently published *Dictionary of National Biography*, seeking out national figures who had been born or brought up in a rectory. The list he produced is remarkable: Ben Jonson, Andrew Marvell, Horatio Nelson, Sir Joshua Reynolds, Jane Austen, the Brontes, Cecil Rhodes, to name a few. With the exception of Curzon of Kedlestone, all the many figures he cited come from the middle classes and the reason is not difficult to find. The education which the aristocracy accepted as its right was largely wasted upon people who had no need to earn a living: it was unthinkable that the working classes should waste their time in book learning. The children of the rectory, on the other hand, were linked to a system where education was available to whoever wanted it. The outstanding ones – or the children of outstanding parents – took up the offer and profited from it.

It was no intention of Henry VIII, founder of the Church of England, that the priests of that Church should marry. To the contrary, it would encourage the class to breed, he thought – a consummation certainly not to be wished. This did not mean that the celibate priest was expected to be denied human comforts. The 'priest's woman' or in more forthright language, the priest's concubine, was a recognized, if not particularly admired figure in history. Even after celibacy had been enforced on the clergy by Pope Gregory VII in the eleventh century, a clergyman could still gain permission to marry on payment of a fine to a bishop. But no ambitious cleric took advantage of this for such marriages automatically put an end to any hope of preferment. Thomas More, later to be canonised, charitably turned St Paul's dictum on its head. 'It's better to marry than to burn', said Paul giving his lukewarm blessing. Not so, said More, marriage defiled the priest 'more than double or treble whoredom'. Cardinal Wolsey was among those who shared that opinion, certainly there was no check to his career because of his two illegitimate children. The point was : they *were* illegitimate and the good Cardinal could therefore show that he had not broken the letter of the law. There is no little irony in the fact that it was his master's wish to marry that brought about his downfall.

Until the death of Henry VIII, the situation was at least clear-cut: if you wanted to get ahead you did not marry. Thomas Cranmer had a wife whom he had married while abroad in Germany but on being summoned to England to become Archbishop of Canterbury, poor Mrs Cranmer was promptly relegated to the status of 'priest's woman', her existence tolerated as long as it was not evident. A legend grew up that she was moved around the country in a travelling trunk or packing case in which holes had been bored. It seems improbable but there was little doubt that the king, for some inscrutable reason, pretended to be unaware of the married status of his Archbishop.

But after Henry's death, and over the next three reigns, the situation became intolerably confused. Under the boy king Edward VI, the godly example of Martin Luther was the one to be followed, and the clergy flocked in scores to take matrimonial vows. But with the advent of Mary to the throne and the swing of the pendulum towards extreme and orthodox Romanism, all these married couples were, overnight, living in sin, and sin was something Mary I could not tolerate. The married clergy had one of two choices: to put aside their wife or give up their living. Edward VI had been on the throne for six years. Given that in the normal course of events, a married woman would be pregnant every 18 months or less, the tragic situation in which many a married parson found himself is evident. A poignant example of what faced them is provided by the fate Sir John Turnor, 'late Parson of saincte Leonard's in Estcheape of the city of London'. Sir John seems to have aroused the particular ire of the new Roman Catholic dispensation, for unlike many of his colleagues, he was not permitted to make a simple renunciation of his wife. In 1554 he admitted his marriage the year before, to Anne Jordan, described as a widow who was 'now pregnant'. The marriage was immediately dissolved and Sir John was given a humiliating penance:

> 'Upon Monday next, viz the 13 of May 1554, in the parish church of Saincte Leonard aforesaid, when the moste number of peoiple shall be there present, the same Sir John Turnor, having a wax taper burning in his hand, and standing in the body of the church before the face of the people, shall openly and distinctly in a loud voice say and declare unto them as follows.'

What followed was an abject confession of his 'sin' in marrying. Presumably thereafter he was allowed to take up his living again – but nothing is known what happened to the unfortunate Anne Jordan, 'widow'. Some women seem to have been able to make the best of both worlds. When Peter Stancliffe, vicar of West Rudham in Norfolk, was forced to divorce his wife, she promptly married someone else – but remarried Stancliffe after the accession of Elizabeth in 1558 when the position of married priests was again legalized. But even then the situation was by no means clear, as is made evident by Elizabeth's famous insult to the unhappy wife of Archbishop Parker. She had been entertained at the Bishop's palace, and on taking her leave of her hostess said coldly, 'Madam I may not call you: Mistress I will not call you, but yet I thank you'. The probability is that she meant it as a rebuke to Parker in that he failed to realize that what might be legal was not socially acceptable.

The parson's wife, who was to play such a key role in the social life of country districts, is a curiously shadowy figure in history. The first direct references to her are anything but complimentary, although it should be borne in mind that those who chronicled her activities were not only male, but males yearning after an original order. Thus the gentle Isaak Walton, patron saint of anglers, has left an unforgettable but corrosive portrait of the marital state of Richard Hooker, one of the most learned men of his time. Two of Hooker's old pupils called in on him, desiring philosophical discourse, and found him minding the sheep in place of the servant who had been called in by his wife. Later, back in the house, they were still denied conversation because, according to Walton, Hooker had been sent off to rock the cradle of his fractious infant. 'The rest of their visit', said Walton of the two young men, 'was so like this that they staid but till next morning, which was time enough to discover and pity their tutor's position'. One of them, more frank than tactful condoled with the scholarly Mr

Hooker that 'your wife proves not a more comfortable companion, after you have wearied yourself in your restless studies'. William Lynche, rector of Beauchamp Roothing in Essex, was deprived of his living under Mary for being married but restored under Elizabeth, he evidently had reasons for regretting his choice of wife. Hauled before the Archdeacons Court for permitting his wife to dance in an ale-house, he supplied a lamentable catalogue of woes:

'Item that he hath never willed her to daunse hymsellfe

Item that he hathe seene other men kys his wieff after daunsing in the common Alehous

Item that he hathe not seene annye bacheler kys her but thei have daunsed with her

Item that he hathe willed her to comme from thalehous but she praied hym to tarie'

The rumbustious Mrs Lynche admitted her crimes, and seems to have set her husband on the downward path, for the following year the unfortunate Parson Lynche was harangued for 'beynge a druncard' and condemned to stand in Chelmsford market-place dressed in a white sheet.

There was no lack of treatises on how the domestic life of the parson should be conducted. In 1652 George Herbert published *A Priest in the Temple: or the Country Parson, his Character, and Rule of Holy Life* which is not simply a moral homily, but throws light on the social life of a country parsonage in the seventeenth century. Herbert, who might fairly be called the Poet Laureate of the English Church, was no narrow Puritan. He had known the great world: in Walton's words he 'changed his sword and silk clothes into a canonical coat' much to the dismay of his friends, who thought it impossible that a man of his attainments would find intellectual satisfaction as a village parson. In his treatise, Herbert naturally emphasizes the moral duties of the parson but then goes on to pinpoint the particular problems that face a married man with children: he must not stint on charities in order to set money aside for their education. Neither should the children be put to such trades as tavern keeping, for men, or lace making for women (the latter prohibition showing a whiff of Puritanism 'because it serves the vices and vanities of the world'). His house furnishings should be 'plain, but clean, whole and sweet – as sweet as his garden can make for he hath no money for such things, charity being his only perfume'. Food should be plain and wholesome, 'what he hath is little but very good: it consisteth most of mutton, beef and veal: if he adds anything for a great day, or a stranger, his garden or orchard supplies it'. Herbert seems to have believed that the products of the parsonage garden – herbs in particular – have an almost mystic value: 'For salves, his wife seeks not the city, but prefers her own gardens and fields before all outlandish gums', and he follows this with an almost lyrical incantation of English herb names: 'valerian, mercury, adder's tongue, yarrow, melilot and St John's wort made into a salve and elder, camomile, mallows, comfrey and mallowse made into a poultice have done great cures'. The country parson was very well aware of the value of his garden. In a list of his tithe accounts, Parson Golty of Framlingham gives a detailed recipe for the making of gooseberry wine which could be used today.

The learned, slightly eccentric, parson cosily tucked away in his study and poring over old records, one of the great ornaments of the English Church, makes his bow. William Harrison, rector of Radwinter in Essex, was commissioned by Raphael Holinshead to write a *Description of England*, one of the first of the great surveys of the country. Harrison cheerfully admits that he wrote most of the book at his desk:

'I must confess that until now of late, except it were from, the parish where I dwell or out of London where I was born, I never travelled forty miles forthright and at one journey in all my life.'

Nevertheless, though sedentary compared with the great travelling antiquaries like Camden and Leland, his cast of mind was such as to make him worthy to be ranked with them. Curiosity was his distinguishing characteristic, whether observing how an adder carried its young in its mouth, or the nature of modern architecture compared with that of his youth in Henry VIII's day, or types of armour, or layout of gardens, or the laws of England – all was grist that came to his mill. The raw material was turned into a sprightly quirky prose which despite its casual style – that of a man conversing by his fireside – succeeds in covering a remarkable area of ground, presenting a lively and fresh picture of Shakespeare's England. Though much of his text was the product of his study, much too came first-hand from those who sat down at his hospitable table, giving him their own impression of the 'state of Britain'. His point of departure is a passionate patriotism, coupled with a good, sturdy xenophobia. Italy comes in for a particular drubbing from this Protestant parson. England was being ruined by the snobbish practice of sending the sons of noblemen into that sink of iniquity. The honest English workmen 'is merie without malice and plain without inward Italian or French craft or subtiltie'. Even criminals are praised, as long as they are English:

'Our condemned parsons doo go cheerfully to their deaths, for our nation is free, stout, hautie, prodigal of life and blood.'

From his study the scholar parson would frequently cast a beady eye on his parishioners. John Earle, rector of Bishopstone in Wiltshire, had been deprived of his living by the Puritans. In 1618, after his re-establishment, he penned a scathing portrait of a Puritan lady which, with some small changes, is recognizable as a certain type of church-goer down the centuries:

'She is a nonconformist in a close stomacher and ruff of Geneva print, and her purity consists much in her linen. She has left her virginity as a relic of popery and marries in her tribe without a ring. Her devotion at the church is much in the turning up of her eye, and turning down the leaf in her book when she hears named chapter and verse. She loves preaching better than praying. She doubts of the virgin Mary's salvation, but knows her own place in heaven as perfectly as the pew she has a key to. She is so taken up with faith she has no room for charity. She overflows so with the Bible that she spills it upon every occasion, and will not cudgel her maids without scripture.'

The office of parson, having survived the extremes of religious fanaticism in the sixteenth and seventeenth centuries, encountered, in the eighteenth century, the most insidious threat of all – the squirar-chy. Insidious, for it was an attack from within, the parish priest either being humble dependent upon the whim of the local great family or, even more damaging, belonging to that great family himself. In January 1700, the widow of the reverend Charles Adams, late rector of Great Baddow in Essex put on record, in excruciating syntax and remarkable orthography, but with admirable frankness an indication of the casually accepted nepotism which settled the succession in the case of the Great Baddow living:

'Mr Abdy that was the Minister dieid and left my Lady Abdy exetricks & my cosen Jack Niklas is to have his living so he is to goe in to orders with all speid, this good living has mad him declar his resolutions of being A Minister & now his next business must be to get a good fortun with a wife, his parsnig will be a very good provision for A younger brother his own porsion besids.'

The great agricultural reforms of the eighteenth century had not only substantially increased the value of tithes, but also increased the parson's own personal holdings – the glebe. The effect was to increase the attraction of the living, increase the pressure to ensure that it remained in the hands of the squire's family. One wonders what relationship, exactly, existed between Mrs Adams' 'Cousin Jack Niklas' and the Lady Abdy in whose hands lay the gift of the living. More and more the rector was closely related to the squire: more and more the vicar or curate was humbly dependent upon the crumbs that fell from the rich man's table. This Biblical phrased had an almost literal interpretation as Joseph Addison made clear in his spirited attack upon the extraordinary custom whereby the squire's chaplain, granted the honour of dining at the squire's table, was expected to decline the sweet courses and leave the table before the port circulated:

> 'I have often wondered at the indecency of discarding the holiest man from the table as soon as the most delicious parts of the entertainment are served up. Is it because a liquorish palate, or a sweet tooth is not consistent with the sanctity of his character? ... Is there anything that tends to incitation in sweetmeats more than in ordinary dishes?. I know not which to censure, the patron or the chaplain: the insolence of power or the abjectness of dependence'.

This was the period when the squire's pew evolved into a private chamber for himself and his family, where shielded from the vulgar gaze – and frequently invisible to the officiating parson himself – they could indulge themselves in what social activities they pleased. One squire even had his letters and newspaper delivered to him in his pew so that he could while away the tedium of the service in their perusal. But this was the period, too, when there emerged one of the most delightful portraits of the squire, fictional though based on fact: Addison's Sir Roger de Coverley.

Addison was himself a child of the rectory, his father holding a poor living in Westmoreland. His description of a country Sunday springs from personal experience, and as with everything he wrote, the elegant language and deceptive casualness conveys a profound truth – one which holds as true today, *mutatis mutandis,* as in the eighteenth century:

*The subservient parson: 'The Vicar going to dinner with the Esquire',
by John Collett 1768.*

'I am always very well pleased with a country Sunday and think,
if keeping holy the seventh day were only a human institution,
it would be the best method that could have been thought for the
polishing and civilizing of mankind. It is certain the country
people would soon degenerate into a kind of savages and barbar-
ians were there not such frequent returns of stated time in which
the whole village meet together with their best faces, and in their
cleanliest habits, to converse with one another upon indifferent
subjects ... Sunday clears away the rust of the whole week: it puts
both the sexes upon appearing in their most agreeable forms, and
exerting all such qualities as are apt to give them a figure in the
eye of the village.'

In a tightknit village society harmony between parson and squire was
essential and Addison describes the parlous state of a village where the
squire and the parson were feuding:

'The parson is always at the 'squire and the 'squire, to be
revenged, never comes to church. The 'squire has made all his
tenants tithe stealers while the parson instructs them every
Sunday in the dignity of his order ... Feuds of this nature, though
too frequent in the country, are very fatal to the ordinary people:

who are so used to be dazzled with riches that they pay as much deference to the understanding of a man of an estate, as of a man of learning.'

Far different, is the relationship between Sir Roger de Coverley and the parson of his village. Sir Roger makes his bow in Addison's fictitious club the 'Spectator's Club'. He is 56 years old, a gentleman of Worcestershire of ancient lineage, 'cheerful, gay and hearty'. It is said that he was crossed in love by 'a perverse beautiful widow' of the next county and he has therefore never married. But he is certainly no misanthrope:

'His tenants grow rich, his servants look satisfied, all the young women profess to love him, and the young men are glad of his company'.

When seeking an incumbent for his Worcestershire living, he

'desired a particular friend of his at the University to find him out a clergyman rather of plain sense than much learning, of good aspect, a clear voice, a sociable temper and, if possible a man that understood a little of backgammon'

– all qualities, one feels, which were possessed by Addison's father.
Sir Roger conducted himself inside the church, as outside, as a benevolent autocrat, generously donating furnishings but not hesitating to discipline the congregation:

The Hungry Curate:
'humming and hawing to his
drowsy herd'
by Holland, 1790.

'I was yesterday much surprised to hear my old friend in the midst of the service calling out to one John Matthews to mind what he was about and not disturb the congregation. This John Matthews, it seems, is remarkable for being an idle fellow and at that time was kicking his heels for his diversion'.

Irritated by the congregation's irregularity in the responses, Sir John provided every parishioner with a hassock and prayer book at his own expense and even employed in itinerant singing master to instruct them in the Psalms. No one presumed to leave the church until the squire's party had filed out. Addison paints a delightful picture of the autocratic but benevolent father of the community walking down the nave between a double row of his tenants, stopping now and then to enquire as to why a son, or a father or a mother were not in the church, a not very subtle means of reprimand for absence.

Addison pinpoints a phenomenon which is remarked upon again and again by contemporary observers of the eighteenth century Church of England:

'As Sir Roger is landlord to the whole congregation, he keeps them in very good order and will suffer nobody to sleep in it beside himself. For if by chance he has been surprised into a short nap at sermon, upon recovering out of it he stands up and looks about him and if he sees anybody else nodding, either wakes them himself or sends his servant to them'.

An appropriate symbol of the eighteenth century church would have been the monstrous pulpit with its sounding board overhead – surrounded by a somnolent congregation. The sermon, around which the reformation had been built, was devouring itself by its very length. Charles Churchill, a curate at Rainham in Essex for two short years, engagingly remarked of his preaching, 'Sleep at my bidding crept from pew to pew'. John Earle, after having pinned down ' A Puritan Lady' like a lepidopterist, added 'a raw young preacher' to his collection:

'The pace of his sermon is full career, and he runs wildly over hill and dale, till the clock stops him, the labour of it is chiefly in his lungs. . . He preaches but once a year, though twice on Sunday: for the stuff is still the same, only the dressing a little altered: he has more tricks with a sermon than a tailor to an old cloak, to turn it and piece it and at last quite disguise it with a new preface.'

Small wonder that the hour-glass was a prominent object in, and narcolepsy a distinguishing feature of, an eighteenth century church service.

*   *   *

Some time about the year 1809, William Combe, confined within the 'rules' of the King's Bench prison in Southwark for debt, pinned on the wall of his squalid chamber the latest drawing by the highly successful artist, Thomas Rowlandson. Combe, then in his late sixties, had been in the King's Bench prison for 21 years and would remain there for almost as long again. The peculiar laws affecting debtors, however, gave him a considerable degree of freedom, and when the fashionable publisher, Ackermann, was looking for a hack to put together some versions linking a series of plates to be provided by Rowlandson, he thought of Combe. In his time Combe had rubbed shoulders with the wealthy as well as the fashionable, first at Eton, then at Oxford where he had squandered a legacy of £2,000. He had travelled on the continent with Laurence Sterne and on return to England set up his plate as a barrister. He earned much, but spent more: the King's Bench prison was an inevitable result of his life style.

Rowlandson had proposed to Ackermann a series of plates depicting the varying fortunes of a travelling schoolmaster, both he and Ackermann accurately calculating on the current fashion for 'Tours' and travel writing. Combe, in an introduction to the second edition of the unexpectedly successful book, remarked truly enough that:

> 'the following poem, if it may be allowed to serve the name, was written under circumstances whose peculiarity may be thought to justify a communication on them. . . An etching or drawing was sent to me each month, and I composed a certain proportion of pages in verse, in which of course, the subject of the design was included. When the first print was sent to me, I did no know what would be the nature of the subject and in this manner the Artist continued designing, and I continued writing, every month for two years 'till a work containing near ten thousand lines was produced'.

In that casual manner did one of the great caricatures of the English parson come into being. The first plate tacked to the wall before Combe, was entitled, 'Dr Syntax setting out on his Tour to the Lakes'. It is set in a village. In the background is Dr Syntax's parish church: in the foreground he, shabbily dressed, is about to mount a sorry looking nag held by a poverty-stricken groom. Behind, the good

Two views of the parson after Dighton, 1760.
(Left) 'A journeyman parson with a bare existence'
(Right) 'A master parson with a good living'.

doctor's wife nags and scolds. Combe thought, then began to scribble, line after line pouring out on paper. Dr Syntax is reviewing his parlous financial situation:

> 'Of Church-preferment he had none
> Nay, all his hope of that was gone,
> He felt that he content must be
> With drudging in a Curacy
> Indeed, on ev'ry Sabbath-day
> To preach, to grumble and to pray;
> To cheer the good, to warn the sinner
> And if he got it – eat a dinner.
> To bury these, to christen those
> And marry such fond folk as chose
> To change the tenor of their life
> And risk the matrimonial strife.
> Thus were his weekly journeys made,
> Neath summer suns and wintry shade;
> And all his gains, it did appear
> Were only thirty pounds a year.'

Syntax decides to make his fortune by writing a popular travel book and Combe and Rowlandson take him through a number of absurd picaresque adventures, before returning him in triumph. He has achieved the goal of all hungry curates: a living. The last Rowlandson picture shows the good doctor, accompanied in his chaise by his plump and haughty wife, greedily eying the handsome rectory that will now be their home while cheering villagers and obsequious churchwardens welcome their new vicar.

It is a misfortune of the Anglican Church that its nadir as a moral

The Sleeping Congregation: satire by William Hogarth, 1736. The only person fully awake is the clerk, surreptitiously peering at the young woman's bosom.

and intellectual institution should have coincided with the rise of one of the art forms in which the English are supreme: the caricature. While, in Latin countries, anti-clericalism turned the priest into devil, in England it turned the parson into a fool – either irrelevant or greedy or both. Hogarth's 'Sleeping Congregation' shows a church struck with that narcolepsy. The parson himself, with ominously upturned hour-glass, seems scarcely awake as he drones on. With the exception of the Clerk, surreptitiously eyeing the accidentally exposed bosom of a fashionable young woman, every member of the congregation has utterly abandoned himself or herself to slumber. In Rowlandson's 'View of the Interior of St Brenver church, Cornwall' the parson is at last fully awake, delivering his impassioned sermon. But he is the only one listening to it, the congregation engaged in a number of activities, from outright slumber to amused interest in each other. Cruickshank has his parson – a rotund little figure with a well stuffed belly – worsted by the village beldame. He has demanded to know why she is not in church instead of smoking and drinking. Pipe clamped in mouth, gin pot clasped firmly in hand, she regards him contemptuously. Why aren't *you* there, she demands 'Preaching your sarmunt instead of walking about troubling your head with other peoples consarns'. Doubtless, if there had been a Rowlandson or a Hogarth or a Cruikshank in the medieval church to illustrate such abuses as those chronicled by Langland and Chaucer, we might have a different picture of the 'Age of Faith'. As it is, it is the eighteenth and early nineteenth centuries which have been pinned down by the merciless pen of the masters. And with good reason, for the Church that had been created in the fires of martyrdom had evolved into a comfortable means of livelihood for a limited class. William Cowper, not the most obvious radical, sadly observed in a letter:

> 'It is no uncommon thing to see the parsonage house well thatched, in exceeding good repair, while the church has scarcely any other roof than the ivy that grows over it. I could not help wishing that the honest vicar, instead of indulging his genius for improvements by enclosing his gooseberry bushes within a Chinese rail, and converting half an acre of his glebe-land into a bowling green, would have applied part of his income to the more laudable purpose of sheltering his parishioners from the weather during divine service'.

The hunting parson now became part of the rural scene, cutting short the service should it interfere with the serious business of killing foxes. A living now was as likely to be taken up because of its sporting and social possibilities as for its income. An advertisement in *Jackson's Oxford Journal* about the year 1810 makes that point quite clear:

'TO BE SOLD BY AUCTION by Hoggart and Phillips, Old Broad Street, London: the next presentation to a most valuable living in one of the finest sporting counties. The vicinity offers the best coursing in England, also excellent fishing, extensive cover for game and numerous pack of fox hounds, harriers etc'.

And if that were not sufficient to entice a man of the Cloth (with a good fat purse) the auctioneers added a tempting rider 'The surrounding country is beautiful and healthy and the society elegant and fashionable'.

On 25 June 1802 there died, in Seathwaite, the Reverend Robert Walker at the age of ninety-three. In the parish register recording his burial is the simple sentence written by someone who had shared his life: 'He was a man singular for his temperance, industry and integrity'. Wordsworth enshrined him in 'The Excursion':

> 'Stern self-denial round him spread, with shade
> That might be termed forbidding, did not there
> All generous feelings flourish and rejoice.'

His highest income was £17 a year on which he brought up a loving family of eight children. His dress was the same as his parishioners: coarse blue smock, apron, wooden clogs. All his free time was spent teaching and while the children repeated their lesson he would be busy at the spinning wheel. He acted, without fee, as lawyer and scrivener for his illiterate parishioners, and he was brought to the attention of the world only through letters about him that appeared in the *Annual Register* in 1760. He was, as the correspondents said, the Good Shepherd.

It is self-evident that the parsons of the eighteenth century more closely resembled Robert Walker than they did the swearing, drinking, hunting parson of the caricaturists, otherwise the whole structure would have fallen apart. But it was the caricaturists' parson which survived in the popular memory and which, in turn, triggered off the reforms of the late nineteenth century, reforms which placed yet another imprint on the millennium old parish church.

St Mary, Melton Mowbray, Leicestershire.
The county's most magnificent church, much of it dating from
the late thirteenth century.

St Mary and All Saints, Chesterfield, Derbyshire. Famous for its twisted spire, probably caused by the contraction of unseasoned wood.

St Mary, Tetbury, Gloucestershire. Built in 1781, it is a homogenous example of the romantic 'Gothic' fashionable at the time.

CHAPTER IX

DIARY OF A COUNTRY PARSON

The parson in fiction has been a staple of English literature, from Chaucer's gentle portrayal of a 'povre Persoun of a toun' to George Orwell's bitterly corrosive portrait of a snobbish, disillusioned priest in *A Clergyman's Daughter*. But the literate parson himself, the man who possessed simultaneously a desire and an ability to record, and ample time in which to do it, has added richly to our knowledge of the everyday life of ordinary folk. They crowd the shelves thick, their diaries and memoirs; some intended for publication, others simply a means of communing with themselves. For the country parson, though living in surroundings which were by no means uncongenial, must at times have found them irksome. He was, after all, by the very nature of his office, literate, and again by the very nature of that office, spending his life largely among illiterate folk. The diary must have been a welcome means of safe escape.

Separately, the diaries and journals appear simply as segments of English literature of greater or lesser value according to the skill of their writers. Placed chronologically, they have incalculable value, regardless of literary content, for they reflect, in a remarkably unself-conscious manner, what ordinary people were really doing and thinking. Frequently it comes as a surprise to find how grass-root activities and motives are considerably at variance with the grand design put forward by later historians.

Four of these diaries: Josselin's in the seventeenth century, White's and Woodforde's in the eighteenth and Kilvert's in the nineteenth, chart the changing social and religious life of the country, or at least an enduring section of the country, from the storm and tumult of the Commonwealth through to the golden calm of High Victorian England.

Josselin was vicar of the town of Earles Colne, some six miles from Colchester, from 1640 to his death in 1683. He began his diary retrospectively in 1644 'but now henceforward I shall be more exact and particular', maintaining almost daily entries, even when he was on campaign. Throughout the Diary, one is aware of the alarums and excursions as England passes through one of its most traumatic periods, from civil war to the irony of the Restoration. On 18 June 1644 'I was ordered by ye Committee as constant chaplyn to attend upon Colonel Harlakendens regiment and to receive 10s per diem as salaray'. This was remarkably high, working out at £168 a year, as compared with the £80 a year he received in tithes and subscriptions, even though he was actually paid only while attached to the regiments. As befits an East Anglian parson, he is fiercely anti-Royalist, fiercely Puritan, recording with satisfaction how at Stamford: 'We spoyle one of ye church ffeasts this day: people are still for ye old ways.' But Earles Colne, in its turn, suffers from the attention of the enemy: 'The cavaliers plundered us, and mee in particular, of all that was portable.' From his parish, he had a ringside view of the siege of Colchester and the triumph of the Parliamentarians. Nevertheless, he records: 'I was much troubled by the black providence of putting the king to death', and on Oliver Cromwell's death, he simply remarks 'Sept 3. Cromwell died, people not much minding it'.

Josselin was certainly no Vicar of Bray, but equally certainly he managed to hold on to his living despite the most violent changes in the country. A few months after the restoration of Charles II he remarks: 'Strange libels cast about in London against the King . . . a good-natured prince but sadly yoked with foreigners', and thereafter again and again has cause to lament on what he regards as increasing immorality in the country, without doing very much about it: 'Some in towne were digging this Sabbath morning. Lord, wither will this profaneness tend? To flat atheism.' He rails against the rise of Dissent, 'My soul morneth to see how quakers and profaners increaseth', and is prepared to fight for his principles if the cost is not too high. He refuses to wear a surplice, is summoned to the bishop's court and is reprimanded, but not fined. He is truly deeply religious, but with a curiously mechanistic view of morality.

Thus he notes that when he gave his sister 3 shillings, someone who had long owed him £7 paid up, 'I have often observed my liberality returned with gain and advantage', God apparently kept a very close account book, however, for when his baby son died he regarded it as a judgement for his love of chess. Anything can provide grounds for a sermon. When a bee stings him on the nose, 'Lett not sin, oh Lord, that dreadful sting be able to poison me'. He can be coldly practical.

When one of his tenants is unable to pay his rent he notes, 'Huggins is undone', and promptly seizes the wretched man's harvest in lieu. Yet he and his wife fasted two meals each week and gave the meat to the poor.

Despite Josselin's keen interest in national affairs, the Diary minutedly records the mechanics of domestic life with the same admixture of idealism and practicality, 'I was with Thomasin, poor troubled heart. Help her, oh Lord! . . . Bought 12 bushels white oates at 22s 6d' all in the same breath. He is perennially troubled about raising funds. The theoretical value of the living was only £8. 10s. 8d, but that was based on the much outdated 'Valor Ecclesiasticus' and was actually now valued at £80 from a number of sources including £40 in tithes, £23 from the Harlakenden family – the local squirearchy £2 in rents and, £15 in contributions from Earls Colne. Although described as a town, even today its population is only that of a village, and Josselin had endless difficulty obtaining the contribution, although whether from an anti-clerical reluctance on the townsmen's part, or real inability to pay he does not make clear.

Nevertheless, each year he is able to record with satisfaction the steady increase of his estate. He gives permission for a tanner to woo his daughter Jane because 'he was a sober, hopeful man' – and his estate about £500: He forbids another daughter's marriage for the prospective husband, though equally honourable, has little estate and no prospects. Jane's wedding cost him £10 and he gave her £200 in dowry, as well as plate worth £40 – altogether a handsome sendoff for one of seven surviving children. His son, on the other hand is a sore trial, a drunken wastrel.

So the record goes on: pigs are fattened and sold at a nice profit; he studies Hebrew; his sister Mary comes to live as a servant –'but my respect shall be towards her as a sister'; £14.10s is invested in a bag of hops, sent by sea to Sunderland; plague strikes. But the Vicar of Earle's Colne goes forward in increasing prosperity and good health, confident in his relationship with God till his 67th Year, when he is afflicted with what appears to be dropsy. 'God remove the fear of death from me' he writes on 25 February 1681. He worsens rapidly. His children gather round. The Diary entries become short, spasmodic, until the last entry on 29 July 'written in a feeble hand the entry much mutilated', according to the diary's modern editor, but still with its interest in the great outside world as well as preoccupation with local affairs: 'Wee begun harvest . . . God send us . . . Heard all well at London, the German nearly . . . by.' And so it ends. For though he lingered on for another eighteen months or so, he never again picked up his quill, and we can agree with his editor '. . . a kindly if somewhat self-centred figure, with the broken entry we feel with real sorrow that we have parted from a friend'.

If much of the interest in Josselin's diary lies in the way in which he interweaves national – and even international – affairs with parochial matters, the charm of Gilbert White's work lies in the fact that he ignores the outside world entirely and creates, in effect, a miniature universe which is nevertheless precisely accurate in all its parts.

'The parish of Selborne lies in the extreme eastern corner of the county of Hampshire, bordering on the county of Sussex and not far from the county of Surrey. It is about 50 miles south-west of London, in Latitude 51 and near midway between the towns of Alton and Petersfield . . . '

Thus he opens his *Natural History of Selborne* with a precision that can still benefit the modern traveller who, using these 200 year old directions, can pinpoint the little village within moments on the Ordnance Survey map. It is this precision which accounts, in large part, for the undying popularity of a book, whose ostensible subject is the wildlife of an obscure English parish. The *Natural History* has the attraction of any exquisitely worked, tiny object. Endearingly, the writer unconsciously shrinks his scale to match: thus the gentle hills of Sussex become a 'vast range of mountain', the little parish of which he treats is seen as a 'vast district', and he enumerates the 12 neighbouring parishes with proud care as though they were provinces of some rural empire.

Gilbert White was born on 18 July 1720, at Selborne where his grandfather had been vicar, and he died on 26 June 1793 about 30 yards from his birthplace. During his early manhood he was obliged to go on the peregrinations of the scholar in Holy Orders (first as a Fellow of Oriel College, Oxford) and then to the curacies that became available. But he never travelled farther than the Midlands, gravitating again and again to his Hampshire village. He was an Oriel man and the living of Selborne was in the gift of another college. He was offered livings elsewhere but refused them, preferring to accept curacies in the Selborne area. In 1784 he took up residence as curate there and remained in the village for the rest of his life.

'I am, at best, but a venerable vegetable, remaining on the same spot like a cabbage for months on end', he wrote to a friend towards the end of his life. But though his body, by choice, roamed within a few square miles only, his speculative mind ranged endlessly – questioning, observing, recording either in notebooks or in letters to correspondents. For the recording was all. Hilaire Belloc once remarked that the ultimate test of a perfect command of English was the ability to describe how to tie a shoelace without resort to illustration and this, in effect, was what White achieved as one of the earliest of our naturalists. Had he been an accomplished artist it is probable that his writing would have suffered. He had one constant goal – the need to describe the specimen before him in words that would enable his correspondent, not only to see it, but to be able to fit it into that supremely satisfying scientific classification system which the eighteenth century was engaged in making.

But besides the scientific need to describe, White had a deep well of compassion, an ability, rare in his time, to recognize that the nonhuman inhabitants of Selborne shared the same world as the human, and had rights. Sometimes the recognition is subtle, implicit: he tells how one winter he discovered a water rat's burrow well supplied with potatoes, and the reader unconsciously empathizes with the little creature snug in its straw-lined burrow under the frozen fields. Sometimes the description is explicit, as in the tragedy of the hen crow. He describes, with his customary exactness, how a pair of crows nested year after year in a particular oak tree. Then the oak was felled:

'The axe was applied to the butt, the wedges were inserted in the opening, the woods echoed to the heavy blows of the beetle or mallet, the tree nodded to its fall, but the dam sat on. At last, when it gave way the bird was flung from her nest. And though her parental affection deserved a better fate, was whipped down by the twigs which brought her dead to the ground.'

The *Natural History* is written in the form of letters to correspondents. Most of his life Gilbert White had widened his physical horizon by corresponding with fellow naturalists and when he came to write the book, he fell instinctively into the epistolary form that gives the work a kind of artlessness. But he is, in fact, employing the art that disguises art, for there is little doubt that he had publication in mind for a long time, and had a shrewd eye for what the public wanted. In a letter to a brother about the brother's own book he remarked: 'Your bookseller must be consulted a little in the title page and advertisements as he knows best how to throw in little savours and alluring circumstances to quicken the appetite of the buyer.' Gilbert White's own book was a generation in the making, for again and again he put off publication, though urged to publish by his innumerable friends. According to White's great, great-nephew, Rashleigh Holt-White, who published the old man's letters in 1900, he feared that the world would 'laugh at an old country parson's book'. Never was an author more incorrect about his book's reception. As the Warden of Merton College remarked when the book was at last published in 1789: 'It has slipped into the world unnoticed save for a few advertisements. The time will come when everyone will want a copy.'

White's book is concerned almost exclusively with the fauna of Selborne. The few references to human beings are, in the main, concerned with abnormalities – a boy who ate bees, a man with leprosy. Judged on this evidence, the Reverend Gilbert White would seem to be a person with no interest in the human race whatever. But his letters show an entirely different side to his personality. Although a bachelor, he was surrounded by young people (at one stage he calculated that he had 61 nieces and nephews), and he goes to great trouble to keep in contact with them. He is the nicest possible kind of pedagogue. Writing to his nephew Sam, he passes easily from a consideration of Hesiod and Virgil to:

'take two pieces of spunge of equal size, weight and softness and hang them by strings over an upland pond in foggy weather, the one as near the surface as possible and the other several feet above the water. Then I would desire you to squeeze the spunges in the morning and see which produces the most water . . .'

His style in his letters has a gentle humour, touched at times with eighteenth century earthiness. Lamenting the hard winter, he writes:

'My rick is now as slender as a waist of a virgin – and it would have been much for the reputation of the last two brides had their waists been as slender'.

The dominant feature of the eighteenth century village, as it is of twentieth century Selborne is 'a vast hill of chalk rising 300 feet above the village, called the Hanger. The covert of this eminence is altogether beech, the most lovely of all forest trees.' White loved this spot. He and his brother John built a zigzag path up to the summit, creating a simple, effective piece of work whose basic design has remained unchanged for two centuries. The brothers also set up an 'obelisk' or large standing stone: Gilbert White, with his passion for accuracy, would have been amused to know that within a century its origins would be forgotten, and it would be solemnly described as part of a druidical structure.

Throughout the village there lie unselfconscious memorials of the man, all the more poignant and effective because of their apparent fragility. The spring called the Wellhead still produces copious crystal clear water:

'This spring produced, September 14 1781 after a severe hot summer, nine gallons of water in a minute, which is 540 an hour and 12,960 in 24 hours or one natural day'.

In the garden of his house the little brick path which he made because he hated getting his feet wet, still exists, though the bricks can easily be prised from the soft earth. Outside the house, the cobble footpath that cost him exactly £1 to lay, forms a useful and handsome part of the village scene. Immediately opposite his house is the butcher's shop which so distressed him by its appearance that he planted four lime trees 'to hide the blood and filth'. Two of the limes still remain.

House-martins continue to gather under the eaves of his old house, The Wakes, as they did in his day, causing him endless fruitless speculation about where they went in the winter. The Wakes is today a museum, and it is one of the pleasanter ironies of history that this home of a man who never willingly travelled more than a mile or so from his village, should be preserved partly as a memorial to a man who died on the other side of the world – Antarctica. When The Wakes came on the market in 1953 an appeal was made for funds to establish it as a museum. Mr Robert Washington Oates made substantial funds available on condition that part of the house should be used as a memorial to Captain Lawrence Oates the 'very gallant gentleman' who perished during Scott's ill-fated expedition. There is a cheerful incongruity in passing from the rooms devoted to White and the gentle Hampshire countryside, to those on Oates and the hostile Antarctic, the eye moving from fieldmice and robins to penguins, from the elegant furniture of a Georgian parlour to sledges and harpoons.

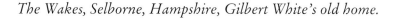

The Wakes, Selborne, Hampshire, Gilbert White's old home.

Despite its proximity to the commuter centres of the Southeast, Selborne probably remains much as White would have known it. The Queen's Hotel, one of the villages two inns, was originally known as The Compasses and was the scene of a remarkably drunken wedding in 1783. White says of it:

'A young, mad-headed farmer came out of Berks to marry farmer Bridgers daughter and brought with him four drunken companions. They set all the village for two days in an uproar. After they drank all the second day at The Compasses they ranted and raved (until) six in the evening. They took the bride (who wept a good deal) and carried her away for Berks. The common people all agree that the bridegroom was the most gentleman of any man they ever saw.'

The old curate was buried in his beloved village, not far from the titanic yew which he described so meticulously. Selborne' burial register for the year 1793 tells a succinct story. On 25 May George Tanner, Senior, was buried 'by me Gil. White, Curate'. So also, on 10 June was Mary Busby, in what seems to have been a season of epidemics, for she was only 16. Then on 1 July is the entry: 'The Reverend Gilbert White, MA aged 72 buried by me Chas Taylor – Vicar.'

In his *Natural History* if not in his letters, White undoubtedly wrote with one eye to posterity. His young contemporary, James Woodforde wrote simply for his own amusement. He was forgotten by everybody for more than a century after his death in 1803, until 1924. That was the year in which James Beresford published the first volume of the five-volume *Diary*. Beresford noted in the one-volume edition of the *Diary* published nine years later:

'The welcome accorded to this obscure country parson, the existence of whose Diaries had been completely unknown even to the Historic Manuscripts Commission, was immediate and widespread. Statesmen, men of letters and that elusive person, the common man all came under Woodforde's spell'.

They continue to do so, for in his ability to speak direct to the reader, the obscure country parson whose death went unmarked by all except his immediate neighbours, is one of the great masters of English prose.

Parson Woodforde is important because he is unimportant, famous because he was never famous, distinguished because he had no

Gilbert White measured the yew tree in front of St Mary's Selborne and found it 23 feet round. It has added about another two feet in the succeeding two centuries.

distinction – save that talent to record in deceptively homely prose the daily life of a handful of ordinary people in a remote agricultural village. The story of the common man is one which tends to go by default, or at best be built up from peripheral documentation. Even in those rare cases where he is the main subject for a great contemporary writer, a Chaucer or a Dickens, he usually serves simply as a model, his story processed into poetry or fiction. But the people in Woodforde's *Diary* are recorded as though with a camera – frozen for eternity into the posture with which they passed through his mind as he was writing up his journal. He was no frustrated artist seeking an outlet: there was no despair, or fear, or stunted ambition that must needs find expression if only through writing. His entries, one feels formed a pleasant, almost automatic habit, a calm review of the day just passed. And they span 43 years.

'I breakfasted, supped and slept at home' is the litany that begins entry after entry, varied only when he is elsewhere on a visit. The village of Weston Longville in Norfolk, where he was vicar for 39 years (37 of which were spent in the actual village) was his world. He was by no means uncultured or untravelled. He was born in Somerset in 1740 and was elected a Fellow of New College, Oxford at 21, subsequently becoming Sub-Warden and Pro-Proctor. He was more fortunate than Gilbert White in that, when a suitable living came up, it was in the gift of his own college. But even after taking up residence

*Parson James Woodforde.
Born Ansford, Somerset in 1740,
he took up living at
Weston Longville, Norfolk in
1766, where he died 37 years later
in 1803.*

at Weston Longville, he frequently returns to Somerset (where he had held various curacies), and often visits London. He hastens to secure copies of *Roderick Random* and *Evelina*, and he is one of the first to read *The Paston Letters* when they appear in Fenn's edition. He is aware of, and records his reaction to, the great issues in the outside world, in particular the violence of the rebels in America and the revolutionaries in France. But it is the woods and fields and villages around Weston that form his universe. The nearest town is the small country town of Reepham some 6 miles away, while Norwich, some 10 miles to the east, constitutes the great metropolis of the villagers' world. Agriculture is the main industry and the overwhelming preoccupation of the villagers, and the *Diary* reflects this. The parson is as often to be found working in his fields or his garden, helped by his man Will, or Ben, or the boy Jack Warton, as he is in his study. Woodforde's meticulous accounts, made up every January, tells us exactly what he paid these helpers annually, and the two maids who ran the house: 'To my head Maid Betty Claxton, £5. 16s; to my Lower Maid Lizzy Greaves £2. 0. 6d.' Will Coleman gets £4, 4s, Ben Leggat, 'my farming man', is paid £10 – a large sum reflecting the importance of his role – and the boy Jack gets 10s 6d. Woodforde presents one penny to each village child, amounting to as much as four shillings in some years (an interesting rule-of-thumb indication of the village's population). Every Christmas Day he has five or six poor old men to dinner. They usually have "a fine surloin of Beef rosted and Plumb Puddings' and he invariably gives them a shilling each.

He receives his tithes in early December and devised a jovial way to take the sting out of the occasion. On each tithe audit he gave what he called a 'Frolick', where everyone ate and drank as much as he could. In December 1782 24 local farmers were entertained to

'some salt fish, a Leg of Mutton Boiled and Capers, a knuckle of veal, a Pigg's face, a fine surloin of Beef rosted and plenty of plumb Puddings. Rum drank, 5 bottles Wine drank 6 bottles besides quantities of strong Beer and ale. Poor John Buck broke one of my decanters'.

In that convivial atmosphere the farmers perhaps scarcely noticed that they had paid £265. 3s in tithes.

Woodforde is a compulsive recorder even when it is probably indiscreet to be so: 'To one Richard Andrews, a Smuggler, for a pound of Tea 9 shillings'. Nothing is too small to be chronicled. On 15 April:

'I told my maid Betty this Morn that the other maid looked so bigg about the Waist that I was afraid she was with Child, but Betty told me she thought not but would inform me if it were so'.

There are no further references to the matter so presumably his

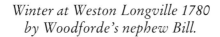

Winter at Weston Longville 1780
by Woodforde's nephew Bill.

gynaecological knowledge was faulty. He must have been very relieved by this for he hated presiding over shotgun marriages, on one occasion recording his dismay and distaste at the fact that the erring young man had been thrown into prison until he decided to do the decent thing.

There is a rather charming relationship with his niece Nancy who lived with him. She kept her own diary, too, and from it we get a cross-reference to life at the rectory. An air of gentle human warmth pervades it. They play cards almost every night for tiny sums, visit neighbours frequently, and gossip much. Nancy is young and so occasionally disposed to rail at her dull village life. Parson Woodforde does his best to enliven things for her. In September 1788 they go on a two-day jaunt to Norwich with friends, his share costing £6,

'It was a dear Frolick but nevertheless I should have been sorry that my niece had not went.'

The reader follows the gradual development of the most important relationship of all – his friendship with Squire Custance of Weston hall. It begins inauspiciously enough:

'June 5 1788. Mr Custance senior called on me this morn – caught me in a very great disabelle and long beard.'

But the two men found much to admire in each other and they successfully establish the delicate relationship between patron and parson, Nancy becoming a particular friend of Mrs Custance's.

Like Josselin before him, Parson Woodforde continued his *Diary* to the end of his life, growing weakness alone forcing him to discontinue it. On 17 October – a Sunday: 'Very weak this Morn, scarce able to put on my cloathes, get down stairs with help.' He noted that the Custances were in church and they had 'rost beef' for dinner. But the rest of the page is blank and thee are no more entries. He died on New Year's Day 1803 and was buried in the beautiful church to which he had, unostentatiously, devoted the greater part of his life.

Despite their great differences in time, space and personality, Woodforde, White and Josselin shared one profound trait in common, a deep involvement in the life of the parish. Each had a strikingly practical, not to say worldly streak, but each was unequivocally the spiritual leader of his little community. Apart from his preoccupation with gaining a living, the reader could be forgiven for not realizing that the Reverend Francis Kilvert was, in fact, in Holy Orders. This was not because he was a worldly young man. To the contrary, he

(Right) Nancy Woodforde, Parson Woodforde's niece, who kept house for him. Three months after his death she recorded:
20 March 1803
'Left Weston Longville this morning where I had lived with my late dear and worthy Uncle 24 years'.

(Left)'Squire Custance'. He and Woodforde successfully maintained the delicate balance between patron and incumbent.

appears in his copious diary as the ultimate romantic, in a permanent state of what seems to be almost painful ecstasy over the beauty of nature and, in particular, the beauty of young women. Were it not, indeed, for his translucently naive nature, his enthusiastic description of little girls might well cause a few eyebrows to be raised. And it is, perhaps, significant that his widow destroyed a substantial part of the diary, and even more of what was left was later destroyed by a niece.

Kilvert must have spent an astonishing amount of time in writing, for even after these successive destructions the diary, which runs only from 1870 to 1879, occupies three fat volumes. Its author was a novelist *manqué*, with a remarkable ability to record atmosphere instantaneously like a camera:

> 'The great round red potatoes lay thick, fresh and clean, on the dark, newly turned mould. I sat down on the stones by the spring and the old soldier came and sat down on the stones with me while his wife went on picking up the red potatoes . . . The spring trickled and tinkled behind us and a boy came from the keepers cottage to draw water in a blue and white jug. . . '

Kilvert, himself the son of a vicar, was curate of Clyro in the Wye valley and so captured the beauties of the area, so identifying himself with it, that since the publication of the *Diary* it has become known as 'Kilvert Country'. But even as late as the 1870's the shadow of a darker past lay over it. Kilvert makes this clear by his curiously casual account of the bestial behaviour of one of the villagers to his daughters, recording a routine sadism with a greater air of detachment than White showed over the fate of a hen crow:

> 'How unkindly their father uses them! The neighbours hear the sound of the whip on their naked flesh and the poor girls crying and screaming when their father comes home late at night. It seems that when he comes home late he makes the girls get out of bed and strip themselves naked and then he flogs them severely or else he pulls the bedclothes off them and whips them all three as they lie together writhing and screaming under the castigation.'

It does not seem to occur either to the Reverend Francis Kilvert, curate of Clyro or to his vicar, Richard Venables, that the three motherless girls were entitled to their protection. On the contrary, the sadist's behaviour seems to have been accepted as a part, if a deplorable part, of village life.

Few of these dark passages are recorded in the surviving part of the *Diary*. Far more characteristic are the accounts of delightful picnics, of long walks in the beautiful Wye valley, of extensive holidays in Cornwall, of balls and parties and dinners. Most of Kilvert's time was spent with the comfortable middle and upper middle classes where he was type cast for the Victorian role of the curate – the handsome, if penurious young man, who could be trusted to squire vulnerable young women while they were waiting for financially acceptable husbands. Twice he stepped out of his role and attempted to become a suitor for their hands, even while aware of his precarious position:

*Francis Kilvert, the young
romantic curate of every
Victorian maiden's dream.*

'On this day when I proposed for the girl who will I trust one day
be my wife I had only one sovereign in the world – and I owed
that'.

On both occasions he was politely, but firmly headed off by the girls'
fathers. His own father promised him that 'one day' he would have
£2,700, but could do nothing to help now, and certainly could not
afford to retire from his own vicarage in favour of his son. Kilvert
approached his vicar who promised to recommend him to the Bishop,
but privately recorded that he would certainly decline the offer of
Clyro itself as a vicarage, giving as his reasons the problem which
would beset endless vicars in the next century:

'I could scarcely keep the poor old vicarage in repair – carpenters
and masons are almost always there to prevent its falling down'.

Preferment did eventually come his way, at the age of 36, so that he
was able to marry three years later. But he died, suddenly, of perito-
nitis a month after marriage.

CHAPTER X

CHANGE AND DECAY?

The eighteenth century was not all torpor and corruption. Indeed, during this very period, when the moral authority of the Church was at its lowest, there occurred the final flourishing of an indigenous church architecture, before the theorists of the nineteenth century tried to lock it into an impossible, ideal 'Gothic' period. The eighteenth century architects of the Baroque, like the nineteenth century architects of neo-Gothic, returned to the past for inspiration. But it was only for inspiration. They did not attempt to copy slavishly, but used the models of Greece and Rome as a point of departure for their own joyous concepts. Hawksmoor, one of the principal exponents of the style, defined his objectives and techniques as following the

> 'rules of the ancients (but) with strong reason and good fancy, joined with experience and trials so that we are assured of the good effect of it'.

London was the principal beneficiary of the new architecture. In 1711, Parliament set up a Commission to superintend the building of 50 new churches in the capital. Parliament's motive was partly to cater for the vast influx of new residents (the population of London trebled in the seventeenth century), but mostly it was a desire to counter the rising tide of Dissent. The Roman Church too, was putting out vigorous new shoots, and it is not without significance that the Commissions's churches reflected the flamboyance of Roman Catholicism rather than the sobriety of the Reformation. One of the members of the Commission, Sir John Vanbrugh, had indeed been a playwright and it is not difficult to see the influence of the stage set in the churches he designed in partnership with Nicholas Hawksmoor.

St Oswald, Ashbourne, Derbyshire. According to George Eliot 'the finest mere parish church in England'.

St Andrew, Alfriston, Sussex. Its proportions, outstanding for a village church, has given it the title of 'the cathedral of the Downs'.

St Pancras, Euston Road, London. Detail of the caryatids.

The magnificent tower and spire of St Mary the Virgin Whittlesey, Cambridgeshire, rise dramatically out of the flat landscape.

The two men worked so closely together that their relationship was a kind of symbiosis. Vanbrugh had had no architectural training and so depended upon Hawksmoor to translate his ideas into reality. But Hawksmoor was an architect in his own right. He had worked with Wren, drawing direct from the master, and the first of the 'Fifty Churches' – St Alfege's in Greenwich – is entirely his own work. The church had been repaired by Wren, but a storm in 1710 brought down the roof, and the churchwardens deciding that its condition was dangerous, applied to Parliament for financial aid. It was probably this which led to the passing of the Fifty Churches Act the following year.

The example set by London was followed throughout the country. This was the period of the Grand Tour when sprightly young men returned home with their heads stuffed full of classical ideals. The family coffers were bulging with revenue from the West Indies, from India, and from the improved farming on their own estates. Most preferred to spend the money on their own homes, pulling down the medieval manor houses of their ancestors to build in the 'correct' new style. But some were also prepared to divert some of the money to the parish church, not always with the happiest result. The church at Great Packington is an extraordinary structure – an attempt to translate the Baths of Diocletian into the English countryside. The architect was an Italian, but he was working under the very close instructions of the lord of the manor, Lord Aylesford, who had visited Rome in 1783. St Peter's in Gayhurst, Buckinghamshire is a happier example: an enchanting Baroque church that is a genuine fusion of styles. In addition, it contains a particularly important funerary monument: the two almost life-size statues of Speaker Wright and his son, the first English commission of the Frenchman, Lois Roubiliac whose work epitomizes the eighteenth century. Cottesbrook church in Northamptonshire provides an excellent example of the squire virtually turning the parish church into a family chapel. Although thirteenth century in origin, the entire interior has been gutted and rebuilt according to eighteenth century canons of good taste. The north transept was demolished, and the south was adapted to make a mausoleum below for the Langham family, and a large, comfortable family pew built on the raised floor.

By the end of the century the movement was exhausted and the Church itself seemed to have become permanently bogged down in a mire of lethargy and corruption:

'Anglicanism was a gentleman's religion, administered by clergy of worldly tastes and ambitions, largely unaffected by the spirit

John Henry Newman (later Cardinal), one of the founders of the Oxford Movement which sought to bring back some of the colourful traditional rituals into the church.

of Christianity. The bishops, nearly all of whom were connected with the aristocracy.... functioned mainly as a power bloc in the House of Lords, wheeling and dealing in the rich emoluments of clerical life. Few of the parsons under their governance bothered with parish duties'.

But in sociology, as well as in physics, every action produces an equal and opposite reaction. The reaction came from the two universities. In Oxford, in 1833, a group of academic clergymen formed an organization later known simply as the Oxford Movement. Colour and life and warmth had gone out of religion, they declared. It was necessary to bring back the rituals of the Old Faith – the vestments, altars, incense, all the things that would restore the sense of awe and mystery to the worship of God. In the fullness of time this movement would develop into Anglo-Catholicism, indistinguishable in the eyes of good Protestants from popery itself. Throughout the century there were to be the most bitter battles between the 'High' and the 'Low' Church, with law suits and even physical violence triggered off by the question as to whether to allow sacred images ('idols' to the orthodox) back into the churches. Missionaries in the slums of the great cities of the kingdom found the trappings of the 'High' Church particularly valuable in drawing potential converts in off the drab streets.

At about the same time as the Oxford Movement came into being, a rather similar organization was born in Cambridge. But where the Oxford Movement debated the question of ritual, the Cambridge

Camden society were pre-occupied by the nature of the building in which such ritual should be enacted. They coined a term 'ecclesiology' to describe their work, and defined it as 'the science of worship carried out in all its material development'. It was these 'ecclesiologists' who, with the best intention in the world, put church architecture into a strait jacket from which it is still struggling to escape. There was only one form of church architecture pleasing to God, they declared, and that was the form evolved in the mid-fourteenth century: the form which Rickman described as 'Decorated', but which the ecclesiologists themselves preferred to call 'Middle Pointed'.

The pre-eminent exponent of neo-Gothic was the splendidly named Augustus Welby Northmore Pugin. The fact that he was a convert to Roman Catholicism adequately sums up his character and his motives. For him, the style in which a church was to be built was not simply an architectural matter. It was theological, for the church was the physical form in which religion presented itself. Classical architecture was pagan; only the Gothic of the Age of Faith expressed the true form of Christianity. In 1835 he published an attractive and witty book called simply *Contrasts*, in which pairs of drawings showed the contrast between the medieval and the modern world. In 'A Catholic town in 1440' the reader is shown an idealized medieval town bejewelled with the soaring towers of great churches. Below is shown 'The same town in 1840'. Gone are the towers, gone the

Shocked members of the Reformed Church saw it drifting back into 'popery' as in this satire from Punch.

churches, gone the rich traceries. In their place are 'the new jail', the 'gas works', the 'socialist hall of science', the whole studded with great chimneys belching forth black smoke.

Even now we are perhaps too close to Pugin to do him justice: had he been born in the Middle Ages, which was his spiritual home, then he could be placed in context. As it is, his incredibly crowded short life – he died at the age of forty – resembles more that of the eccentric so cherished by the English, than that of the genius. He was an original. Before he was fourteen he had thrown himself into designing medieval buildings, before he was twenty he had gained fame as a designer of operatic scenery – a skill which was going to come in very useful when he turned to church architecture. He married twice before he was twenty-one, turned his back on architecture, then picked it up again. Unlike such pedestrian natures as George Gilbert Scott and Thomas Rickman he did not so much copy Gothic styles as re-create them. A Pugin church is instantly recognisable as being of the nineteenth century, yet it is infused with that design associated with the so-called Age of Faith.

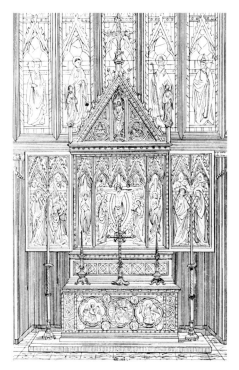

'Contrasted altars' according to Augustus Pugin. As a convert to Roman Catholicism inevitably he looked to the Middle Ages for his inspiration.

By one of the fortunate acts of history Roman Catholicism and Pugin coincided in time. The Catholic Emancipation Act of 1829 allowed Roman Catholics the right to freely practise their religion again. Suppression had not been total. In Birmingham, as in other cities, there had been Catholic chapels where the old rites had been conducted with a certain amount of discretion. A masshouse was built there by a Franciscan in 1688 (its site recorded in the present day by Masshouse Circus on the Ringway), and though it was later destroyed by a Protestant mob, a chapel was eventually built in 1808 on the site of what is now the cathedral. In Burnley, in Lancashire a public chapel replaced a private one in 1817, and a small but handsome little church was built in Willow Lane, Norwich in 1827. But with the Emancipation Act grandeur could replace discretion. One further coincidence gave Pugin the opportunity he needed. The enormously wealthy Earl of Shrewsbury was a Roman Catholic and it was he who financed the building of the Catholic church of St Giles in the small Staffordshire town of Cheadle. Although not particularly large, it is on a superb site rising high in the very heart of the town. No expense was spared in the decorating and furnishing of the interior, and Pugin was able to indulge himself to the full, from the great oaken west doors with their full-size lions rampant of the Shrewsbury arms, to the richly decorated sedilia and piscina in the sumptuous chancel.

The first Anglican church of the new dispensation was All Saints Church in Margaret Street, London. The architect was William Butterfield and he carried into practice Pugin's passionate belief that work was prayer: that the moral attitude of the builder was as important as his architectural skill. Both in the drawing office and on site, the conduct of Butterfield's workers more closely resembled that of monks than of lay builders. It was axiomatic that they were practising churchmen, but even in their working hours silence prevailed, except when it was time for prayers. Whether or not the pious discipline produced the result, Butterfield's church is a great work of art. The exterior is somewhat startling, a riot of multicoloured tiles and bricks whose polychrome impact has survived even a century of London soot. But the interior is deeply satisfying in its solemnity and richness of colouring.

Now the great age of church building was launched, a period which outstripped even that of the thirteenth century. Parliament started the process with the Church Building Act of 1818, providing for over 200 churches to meet the sudden urban expansion of population consequent upon the Industrial Revolution. Private builders followed: every architect worth his salt was ensured an ecclesiastical commission, and it has been calculated that about half of the surviving parish churches of England were built after 1820. The vast majority were in the now mandatory neo-Gothic style. In the hands of the founders of the movement, men like Butterfield and Pugin, Scott and Pearson (who habitually took the Sacrament before he started work), the anachronistic style produced great buildings. But as the decades wore on, in the hands of lesser men, the style was watered down, became boring, mechanistic, predictable. Inexperienced churchwardens, faced with the need to decide on the style for an extension or a rebuilding, more and more opted for the 'Gothic' style that had had the blessing of the learned, the pious, and the great. And the 'architects' who worked for them, using standardized form books, unthinkingly used the style whether or not it was appropriate to the task. But worse, far worse was to come.

The sensitive visitor to an ancient church has learned to dread the phrase, 'restored in 1880' or thereabouts, which occurs in so many guide books. In their quest for the ideal architecture the ecclesiologists were not simply content to build new churches, but wanted to 'restore' old churches, stripping off all the accretions of any centuries later than the idealized fourteenth. They were aided and abetted by 'progressive' parsons. The peculiarly Anglican system of Church preferment means that, within the confines of his parish, the parson is virtually pope. In a symposium on the subject of modern church restorations, the Very Reverend Tony Bridge made the point that

> 'until this century clergy have often treated their churches, *de facto* if not strictly *de jure*, as places which were as much theirs to do with as they liked as their vicarage or even their potting sheds.'

Throughout the nineteenth century, disastrously energetic parsons were ripping out 'debased' architectural forms in pursuit of the pure 'Gothic' which fashion decreed was the only form pleasing to God. This destructive freedom possessed by every incumbent was only too well illustrated by the reported case of the Lincolnshire church

> 'which was restored throughout in the most approved fashion, except that the very ancient Norman chancel arch was for a time spared. It remained not long, for the young ladies of the Parsonage could not bear to see it. They found it so wholly out of keeping and frightfully disfiguring to the new work, and so it was taken down'.

To the long list of hazards that faced ancient churches was now to be

St Augustine's, Kilburn, London,
the epitome of the Age of Confidence.
Its architect, John Pearson, took the Sacrament before
commencing work.

added bored young ladies, turning from painting on velvet to architectural criticism.

The report of the depredation of the Lincolnshire church was made by a speaker at a meeting of the Society for the Protection of Ancient Buildings. Founded in 1877 by William Morris, the Society (which still survives) was a vigorous reaction against that wave of 'restoration' which was disfiguring the churches of the country. In a resounding manifesto Morris indicated the reason for the Society's existence, and the course it would take, and in so doing he summed up the dizzying eclecticism and uncertainty of direction which prevailed, not only in his own time, but down to today:

> 'The civilized world of the nineteenth century has no style of its own amidst its wide knowledge of the styles of other centuries. From this lack and this gain arose in men's minds the strange idea of the restoration of its ancient buildings: and a strange and most fatal idea, which by its very name implies that it is possible to strip from a building this, that and the other part of its history, of its life that is, and then to stay the hand at some arbitrary point and leave it still historical, still living and even as it once was.'

If the term 'twentieth' is substituted for 'nineteenth' in Morris's manifesto it is applicable to our own time. Indeed, it is perhaps even more relevant as the descending curve of church attendance meets the rising curve of antiquarian conservationism, leaving us with an increasing number of well preserved historic buildings for which there is no obvious function. In town churches, one of the most powerful, personal links between the community and the parish church was severed with the cessation, in the nineteenth century, of burials in the churchyard. In the 1930s, in particular, there arose a regrettable obsession for 'tidying up' and for transforming the churchyard into an 'amenity'. Tombstones were moved and lined up neatly against walls as decorative features, suburban plants introduced. In the postwar years the ubiquitous petrol-driven 'strimmer' destroys the variegated wildlife, reducing the grass again to suburban neatness.

Churches have been further moved out of ordinary daily life by the every increasing custom of locking the doors. This is not a new problem. In the late nineteenth century the naturalist, W. H. Hudson, described a conversation he had with the vicar of the tiny little church of Coombe, in Cornwall

> 'He assured me that he had never once locked the church in fifty years: day and night it was open to anyone to enter. It was a

refuge and shelter from the storm and tempest, and many a poor homeless person had found a dry place to sleep in that church . . . But how strange all this would sound in the ears of many country clergymen. How many have told me when I have gone to the parsonage to 'borrow the key' that it had been found necessary to keep the church locked to prevent damage, thefts etc'.

There is admittedly greater need today to foil the sophisticated theft of the antiques in which our churches abound. The present writer, visiting a suburban church, was surprised to find himself closely questioned by a lady arranging flowers. It transpired that the previous week, when the flower arrangers had retired for coffee, leaving the church unlocked for a quarter of an hour or so, a large, valuable 'Parliament' clock had been skilfully removed: 'The police told us that it would be on the continent by nightfall'. Care is necessary, but it does seem to be carried to extremes. On a busy autumn Saturday afternoon every church in central Ipswich was locked although all were fully in view of hundreds of people.

Apart from the decline in religious belief, the overwhelming problem facing most of our churches is the relocation of population. Since 1968 the Church Commissioners have declared over 500 churches to be redundant. The problem is particularly acute in the great historic cities of the country. In Norwich there are some 35 important churches within the city walls, but probably less than a quarter of the population live within those walls. The glorious Wren churches of the City of London stand forlorn and empty two days out of seven, and every evening. In recent years there have been systematic attempts to find appropriate uses for churches whose population has left them. One obvious use is to cede the historic redundant churches to another denomination, but in the past, there has been something of a dog in the manger attitude to this idea. In 1952 the ancient church of St Jude in Elm Hill, Norwich, became redundant. Local Roman Catholics wanted to acquire it as their own parish church, but were refused, and the church was converted into a Scout's meeting hall. That attitude is happily in the past: in the same city the church of St John Maddermarket is now used by the Greek Orthodox Church.

The most famous example of a new use for an old church is that of St John's, Smith square, London. Bombed during the War, it was restored as a concert hall. There are many more excellent examples of such conversions into other dignified uses. In Oxford, All Saints has been turned into a superb library for Lincoln College. St Andrews in Chichester, a forlorn, dilapidated building a few years ago, is now a handsome arts centre; St Sampson's in York is an old people's day centre. St Peter's Church in Marlborough, built in 1450, was actually condemned to demolition in order to create a traffic roundabout. Energetic action on the part of Marlborough citizens not only saved the church, but with the help of a grant of £40,000 from the Department of the Environment turned it into a flourishing Arts Trust.

The State aid given to St Peter's marks one of the most important developments in church maintenance. In the past, there has been considerable reluctance on the part both of State and Church, to allow the State to become financially involved in the running of churches. The homely proverb 'he who pays the piper calls the tune' explains the Church's reluctance, while the State is not over keen to have the burden of maintenance costs and the increasing number of historic churches becoming redundant urgently required a solution. A partial solution was found in 1968 with the setting up of the Redundant Churches Fund. According to its Secretary, John Bowles:

> 'The Fund is a unique partnership between Church and State, funded by both yet independent of both as a statutory body. In addition to its statutory independence it is distanced from controversy by the fact that it has no say in the choice of churches placed in its care, apart from a financial one'.

John Bowles insists that the Fund is 'not looking after ecclesiastical mini-museums'. All the 238 churches in the care of the Fund are consecrated buildings, most being used for services at least once a year. The tiny little Saxon church at Albury, in Surrey, for instance, regularly holds a service on the Sunday nearest to Midsummer Day, preceded on the previous night by a concert of music and poetry.

The current emphasis on church maintenance, the endless appeals for money to repair the roof, repair the tower, repair the organ, and the rise of a purely antiquarian interest, would seem to argue that the church has joined the temple in the museum of history, its religious significance important only to a minority – and an ever decreasing minority. In recent years, however, the rise of an astonishing phenomenon – the phenomenon of pilgrimages – gives this the lie. It is a remarkable, nationwide renaissance in a country which was not only in the forefront of the sixteenth century Protestant reaction against 'Popish practices', but is also increasingly stigmatized as being irreligious. The ancient focal points have come to life again: St Albans and Canterbury, Ripon and Holywell. Even the tiny shrine in Bawburgh, Norfolk, dedicated to the eleventh century farm-labourer saint, Wulstan, now sees its regular pilgrimages.

The Slipper Chapel, Walsingham, Norfolk:
one of the few Pre-Reformation elements of the Shrine surviving
intact. Pilgrims removed their shoes here to walk the last mile
into the village.

Interior of the Anglican shrine at Walsingham.
Behind the altar is a reconstruction of the Holy House of Loreto.

The doyen of them all is Walsingham, and the experience of this little village in Norfolk epitomizes the movement. Something decidedly odd has twice happened in Walsingham, once in the eleventh century, and once again 900 years later. Some time about the year 1050, the lady of the manor, a certain Richeldis, had – or claimed to have had – a vision in which the Madonna instructed her to build a replica of the Holy House of Nazareth, in Walsingham.

The nature of the vision has been debated for centuries. Whatever its origins, it was powerful enough not only to create one of Europe's foremost shrines, second only to St James of Compostella, in Spain, but to survive four centuries of suppression, before bursting into an astonishing efflorescence in our own time, providing a stimulus for other shrines to follow.

Suppressed by Henry VIII, the shrine was restored in the 1920s by a charismatic Anglican priest, Arthur Hope-Patten, in the teeth of orthodox opposition. The first pilgrimages, numbering a few hundred, took place under the disapproving gaze of the Bishop of Norwich and his fellow prelates. By contrast, in 1980 the Archbishop of Canterbury and the Cardinal Archbishop of Westminster jointly led a pilgrimage of thousands. Annually, some 250,000 people visit this small village, causing severe crises of hygiene at peak periods.

Modern pilgrims follow the path of their medieval predecessors. About a mile outside the village is the exquisite fourteenth century Slipper Chapel, the only intact survival from the Middle Ages. Traditionally, this is where pilgrims removed their shoes to walk the

*Memorial of
Bishop Stephen O'Rorke
in the Anglican shrine at
Walsingham.*

last mile barefoot – Henry VIII was one such, and the more devout pilgrims still do. The chapel was the centre of the Roman Catholic pilgrimages until 1981, when an immense, handsome austere new building was consecrated. It can seat 700 or accommodate an open air congregation of 10,000, setting a potent example of the modern drawing power of the ancient shrine.

Beyond the Slipper chapel the Vale of Walsingham rises on each side of a little bubbling river, the Stiffkey. The titanic remains of the medieval priory in the middle of the village are on private lands, but access is permitted on payment of a modest sum. It is one of the focal points of any organized pilgrimage, with thousands pouring in to stand where their predecessors stood five centuries ago. But it is the Anglican shrine which is the high point of the village. Largely Hope-Patten's concept, it was a deliberate attempt on his part to create a devotional atmosphere. The interior of the church is dizzyingly eclectic, drawing freely upon Byzantine or Norman, or medieval English or Italian sources. It would be dramatic in Rome, startling in London. In a Norfolk agricultural village it simply stuns the imagination.

Inside, its central feature is a replica of Richeldis's Holy House based on contemporary descriptions of the original. Erasmus was one of the hundreds of people who visited the shrine before its suppression, and though he left a sardonic account of the vial of the Virgin's milk, which was supposed to be venerated, he left a very useful description of the Holy House which served as a guide for its rebuilding in 1931. It is a plain, hut-like structure, studded all over with stones taken from other shrines, its interior blazing with flickering candlelights so that the looming image of the Madonna, based on the Great Seal of the Prior of Walsingham, takes on a life of its own. One wonders what Erasmus would make of it all today.

APPENDIX

Select list of churches arranged chronologically

Astonishingly, no one knows exactly how many churches there are in Britain. *Crockford's Clerical Directory,* the 'Bible' of the Anglican Church, gives a comprehensive list of parish churches. But only of Anglican parish churches, non-Anglican churches and chapels and redundant churches being ignored and non-parish churches being placed as subsidiary to parish churches whatever their historic merit. A rough calculation places the total number of churches in England at around 20,000 with about half being recognized as possessing historical interest.

The list that follows attempts to give a cross-section of historical forms. Rickman's classification, sanctified by use if not by logic, forms the core of this classification but it has been extended to include forms developed after Rickman.

As explained in Chapter II it is impossible to give a single, firm date for a building which may have been in used over centuries. In this listing, a church has been allocated to a particular section of the list depending upon its possession of an important architectural feature which has happened to survive, such as the crypt of Repton in Derbyshire. Or the fact that certain elements of the building mark a moment of change. Thus the church of All Hallows in London, though of Saxon foundation and with one or two Saxon and Norman survivals, and substantially rebuilt after World War II, has been placed in the seventeenth century when its unique Cromwellian tower was built and Grinling Gibbons designed its font cover.

The list stops at 1900. Since World War II some of the most interesting urban architecture has been ecclesiatic, Noncomformist chapels in particular. But as yet no clearcut pattern on the 'Rickman' model has emerged to create a framework.

SAXON

Bradford-on-Avon, Wiltshire
St Laurence

Founded some time before 709. Perhaps the most perfect Saxon survival in England and owing that survival to accident. Abandoned after the parish church of Holy Trinity was built in the twelfth century, it was put to secular use for a long time before its history was unearthed by an antiquarian parson of the nineteenth century.

Brixworth, Northamptonshire
All Saints

Founded *c.* 675. Originally a monastic church, it became a parish church some time after 870 when the rest of the monastery was destroyed by the Danes. One of the largest of the Saxon churches, a considerable quantity of Roman building material was used in its construction.

EARLS BARTON, NORTHAMPTONSHIRE
All Saints

Early eleventh century. The characteristic Saxon 'long and short work' (ashlar blocks designed to strengthen the corners of rubble-built walls) has here been made an art form in its own right. The otherwise plain, square tower has been made spectacular, the ashlar strips being used decoratively as well as functionally.

GREENSTED, ESSEX
St Andrew

Founded 1013. The world's oldest wooden church, surviving the drastic 'restoration' of the nineteenth century. Built as a resting place for the body of King Edmund on its way to Bury St Edmunds. The nave walls consist of the original oaken logs, adzed and placed on a wooden sill.

REPTON, DERBYSHIRE
St Wystan

The church itself was built in the tenth century, but its most interesting part is the crypt which was originally built as a mausoleum for the royal house of Mercia. Wystan, heir to the throne, was buried here in 850, his tomb subsequently becoming a shrine. The crypt was accidentally discovered in 1799.

MONKWEARMOUTH, TYNE & WEAR
St Peter with St Cuthbert

Founded in 674 by Benedict Biscop, credited with being the first person to build in stone – a skill he brought back with him from the Continent. Originally part of a monastic establishment, it became a parish church after the Dissolution.

SOMPTING, WEST SUSSEX
St Mary

Early eleventh century. Famous for its remarkable tower which quite dwarfs the church. Based on Rhenish models, this was the nearest the Saxons ever came to creating a spire.

WORTH, W. SUSSEX
St Nicolas
Although caught up in the suburbs of Crawley St Nicolas still retains

its identity in its ancient churchyard. It is not clear why this immense pre-Consquest church was built in what was simply a forest clearing although it was probably related to the saxon royal house. The tower is nineteenth century (by Salvin) and the roof restored after a disastrous fire in 1986 but this is still a Saxon church, built on the same monumental scale as All Saints, Brixworth.

NORMAN/TRANSITIONAL

Barfrestone, Kent
St Nicholas

The outstanding feature here is the extraordinary tympanum of the south door of the nave. Built about 1170, it is a riot of carving that gives the lie to the usual picture of the Normans as a dour and unimaginative race. The central figure shows Christ in the act of blessing, enclosed in arches on which are depicted both biblical and everyday scenes.

Castor, Cambridgeshire
St Kyneburga

The massive tower, with its rich arcading was built in 1124 and would have been a dignified addition to a cathedral. Its appearance here is testimony to the past importance of the small village of Castor now threatened with engulfment by Peterborough. The Norman church survives within a shell of later developments.

Kilpeck, Hereford & Worcester
St Mary and St David

Although built about 1134, two full generations after the Norman Conquest, this little church still shows signs of the Saxon influence which long survived in this part of the country. One of the smallest churches in England it is one of the most richly decorated with a wealth of sculpture, including the extraordinary fertility figure know as the *sheil-na-gig*.

London, Smithfield
St Bartholomew the Great

Founded *c.*1103 by Rahere, courtier of Henry I, as part of a priory in thanksgiving for recovery from malaria. Priory and nave were demolished after the Dissolution but choir and transepts survived to become a parish church. Rahere's ornate tomb dates from the fifteenth century.

LONDON, FLEET STREET
Temple Church

A textbook example of the Transitional style. The round, modelled on the Holy Sepulchre Church in Jerusalem as were all Templar churches, was consecrated by the Patriarch of Jerusalem in 1185. The great west doorway, with its richly carved orders, is entirely Norman. Inside, the clerestory and aisle windows are rounded in the Norman style – but the arches of the main arcade are in that pointed style later to be known as Gothic. Above eye level the triforum arcading is entirely Transitional with pointed arches resting on columns of Purbeck marble – one of the earliest uses of that marble in England.

PYRFORD, SURREY
St Nicholas

The prominent siting of this church on an isolated knoll argues that its foundation is of very great antiquity, an excellent example of a church being placed on an existing *ciric*, or holy ground. The present church was built about 1140. It contains some of the country's oldest murals, contemporary with the building of the church, and discovered in 1967.

EARLY ENGLISH (1175-1275)

EATON BRAY, BEDFORDSHIRE
St Mary

A fifteenth century exterior hides a remarkable early thirteenth century interior. The north and south aisles with their superb piers each with its elaborately carved capital were built between 1220-1250. The richly carved font and the intricate ironwork of the door all date from the same period.

KETTON, LEICESTERSHIRE
St Mary

Transitional between Rickman's Norman and Early English. The west front is late twelfth century but the austere majestic tower soaring above the village is entirely thirteenth century. The graveyard contains some outstanding carved tombstones.

NEWARK, NOTTINGHAMSHIRE
St Mary's

A superb town church which owes its grandeur to the fact that Newark possessed only one parish and St Mary's became the focal point of the entire community. The great tower is transitional from the elegance of Early English to the comparative floridity of Decorated.

West Walton, Norfolk
St Mary

A perfect Early English church, reflecting the county's wealth at this time. Nave, aisles, piers and chancel of this mid-thirteenth century church are entirely homogenous. There are remains of murals of the same period. Even the detached tower is of the same date.

Whitchurch Canonicorum, Dorset
St Candida

The only church still containing the relics of a saint, the so-called 'St Wite', though shrine and church were built long after his/her supposed lifetime. The main body of the church dates from the late twelfth/early thirteenth century. The shrine, with apertures into which the afflicted thrust an arm or leg (or article belonging to a sick person) is thirteenth century.

DECORATED (1250-1350)

Cley next the Sea, Norfolk
St Margaret

The clerestory, aisle windows and exterior crenelation of this delightful little seaside church does warrant the description 'decorated'. The small secondary tower or turret acted as a lighthouse.

Uffington, Oxfordshire
St Mary

The parish church of Tom Brown of *'Tom Brown's Schooldays'*. Mostly early thirteenth century, rather bleak inside but with an unusually rich priest's door and remains of fifteenth century screen. The eighteenth century added another storey to the tower but forebore to embellish it.

Leominster, Hereford & Worcester
St Peter and St Paul

A good example of part of a monastic complex which physically survived the Dissolution of the Monasteries. Although much of the priory church was demolished, the nave which had always been used as a parish church, emerged into independent life, though with considerable additions.

BRISTOL, AVON
St Mary Redcliffe

This cathedral-like church was built, one feels, less to the greater glory of God than to the glory of the Bristol merchants whose wealth created it. 'The fairest, goodliest and most famous parish church in England' was the verdict of Elizabeth I, no mean judge of architecture. It is particularly famous for its splendid stone vaulting.

WITNEY, OXFORDSHIRE
St Mary the Virgin

Although heavily restored in the nineteenth century St Mary's still clearly shows its ancestry, including some Norman remains. The tower and spire are pure thirteenth century. There is a typically elegant Decorated monument (of a priest, believed to be the founder) in the north transept.

PATRINGTON, N. HUMBERSIDE
St Patrick

In order to build this 'Queen of Holderness' at the turn of the thirteenth/fourteenth centuries, an existing church that had itself only recently been completed was demolished – evidence at once of the wealth produced by the Humber trade and the priority given to church building. It possesses one of the surviving Easter Sepulchres.

PERPENDICULAR

BOSTON, LINCOLNSHIRE
St Botolph

This church sits on the boundary between Rickman's classifications of Decorated and Perpendicular. The nave is of the fourteenth century as is evident from its windows, but the famous Stump is Perpendicular. The Stump is almost too successful for it overwhelms the rest of the church. Viewed from outside the nave appears almost as an appendix and its true grandeur is revealed only inside.

FOTHERINGHAY, NORTHAMPTONSHIRE
St Mary and All Saints

Viewed from across the rich green meadows the church has an extraordinary truncated appearance – a dwarf wearing giant's robes – for its massive, majestic tower looks as though it should belong to a far larger building. The church was once part of a college of priests, the rest of the building falling victim to the Dissolution of the Monasteries. The college itself was once attached to Fotheringhay Castle, where Mary Queen of Scots was beheaded. The castle was demolished in revenge by Mary's son James I and only a few earthworks remain.

LONG MELFORD, SUFFOLK
Holy Trinity

A classic Perpendicular church, whose slender elongated features perfectly illustrate why Rickman chose the term 'perpendicular' for this period of architecture. Characteristic also is the remarkably high proportion of glass to stone, so that it seems as though the building is simply a framework for the windows.

SAFFRON WALDEN, ESSEX
St Mary the Virgin

The perfect town church. Set in a green space in a slightly elevated position in the heart of the town, but tucked slightly to one side so that it adds dignity, but does not dominate. As with many churches, the upper chamber of the south porch was used as a school room.

CIRENCESTER, GLOUCESTERSHIRE
St John the Baptist

Like the Boston Stump, one feature virtually overwhelms the rest of the church. In this case it is the incredible porch. Erected about 1490, it is a three-storey building in its own right and reaches more than halfway up the tower – itself an impressive structure. It was, in fact, the fifteenth century equivalent of an office block, for its upper storeys were used for administrative purposes.

BLYTHBURGH, SUFFOLK
Holy Trinity

Some of the most splendid of Perpendicular churches occur in East Anglia – testimony to the wealth of the region. Holy Trinity has visually gained in status, for Blythburgh today is little more than a village with no other building to compete with Holy Trinity's majesty. Puritan iconoclasts did their best to disfigure it as testified by the bullet holes in the beautiful angels of the roof. The chamber above the porch is still in regular use

THE AGE OF REFORM (1600-1800)

(Rickman's classification ends with Perpendicular *c.*1550. Church building virtually ceases with the uncertainties following the Reformation. When it begins again it is in an entirely new form with preaching taking precedence over ornament, reason over mystery).

LONDON, COVENT GARDEN
St Pauls

In designing his church (building commenced in 1633) Inigo Jones, the architect, had to create a balance between giving dignity to the House of God and not offending the godly by adding 'superstitious' ornaments. Nevertheless, liturgy affected the design for Jones intended the entrance to be from the piazza on the east and placed his main portico there, but Archbishop Laud insisted the entrance must be from the west. The great portico is therefore in the wrong place.

LONDON, WALBROOK
St Stephen

It is easy to pass this by so hemmed in is it now, but even when Wren designed it in 1672 he had no alternative but to tuck it away on an awkwardly shaped site that inevitably became obscured. But the moment you step in 'the triumph of reason over superstition' becomes evident. Mystery has been banished. Despite its grandeur this is, essentially, a debating chamber.

LONDON, CHEAPSIDE
St Mary Le Bow

Probably the best loved, certainly the best known of all Wren churches associated as it is with 'Bow Bells'. Begun the year before St Stephen's it occupies a prominent site and Wren made the most of this by designing for it his most distinctive steeple. The interior was totally gutted by fire during World War II and has been redesigned in a modern manner which has attracted considerable criticism.

LONDON, BYWARD STREET EC3
All Hallows by the Tower.

This is a church that makes a mock at any attempt to slot it into one fixed period. In its crypt are the remains of a Roman mosaic and Saxon tombs: its tower was built in the time of the Commonwealth when church building was virtually at a stand-still; the interior, after being gutted by air raids in World War II, unabashedly uses ferro-concrete and a modern design and modern sculptures decorate the interior. But the pulpit, probably by Wren (from the demolished church of St

Swithin) and Grinling Gibbons' enchanting font cover are among the elements which help to place it in this period.

LONDON, CITY
St Mary Woolnough

Built by Nicholas Hawksmoor between 1716 and 1727 under the Fifty Churches Act of 1711. Here 'reason' has been taken to extreme lengths. Where Wren subordinated design to the 'idea' of debate, Woolnough gave it full reign. The massive, solid front of the church is an exercise in mathematics which, for all its brooding power, is reminiscent of a child's box of bricks.

NORWICH, NORFOLK
The Octagon Chapel

The idea introduced by Wren of the congregation meeting for instruction, rather than worshippers come to celebrate a mystery, is carried to its logical conclusion in this beautiful austere building. It is a meeting place rather than a church. Designed by Thomas Ivory and built in 1766 it is an eight-sided structure in brick whose elegantly panelled interior, with its eight Corinthian columns, seems curiously larger than indicated by its exterior.

PETERSHAM, SURREY
All Saints

Although it can trace its origins to the thirteenth century this is essentially a Georgian church, as is proved by the return of decoration. Preaching is still a primary function but the elegant ballustrade of the steps leading up to the pulpit and the highly coloured royal coat of arms betoken a frivolity that would have shocked the Puritans.

THE AGE OF CERTAINTY (1800-1900)

LONDON, EUSTON ROAD
St Pancras

Built between 1819 and 1822, its architect, Willam Inwood, not only distanced himself from the Christian Reformation but returned to the pagan classic past for his inspiration. The tower is a copy of the Tower of the Winds of Athens and on either side of the east end is a copy of the Porch of the Maidens on the Acropolis, complete with life-sized – rather bulky Maidens – in terracotta. St Pancras is the forerunner of that Greek Revival which will be immensely popular in the next half century.

BRIGHTON, SUSSEX
St Bartholomew

Built in 1876, the pendulum has begun to swing strongly towards the Gothic. The architect, Edmund Scott, was executing the liturgical intention of the Anglo-Catholic Movement where the church again becomes a stage for the enactment of a mystery. To hammer home the point the high altar is virtually enclosed by the pillars of an immense *baldachino*, creating an inner sanctum.

ROKER, TYNE & WEAR
St Andrew

Ironically, the architect of this splendidly craggy Gothic building was E.S. Prior. Ironical, because Prior propagated the myth that there were no 'architects' in the Middle Ages, the great churches and cathedrals growing virtually organically: 'the determiner of their forms of beauty did not exist in any personality'. St Andrew, built between 1905 and 1907 has been called 'the cathedral of the Arts and Crafts movement', many of its internal decorations coming from the hand of artists such as Eric Gill and William Morris.

LONDON, KILBURN
St Augustine

The Victorian Gothic architect only too often exercised his belief that he knew more about Gothic buildings than their original builders by ruining the work of his predecessor. The architect of St Augustine's, John Loughborough Pearson, had an absolutely clean slate on which to express his ideals. This stunning church is the result. Commenced in 1871, although the structure itself was completed in 1898, the elaborate decorations went on for many more years. By the time they were complete, doubt and uncertainty about the shape a church should take reflected uncertainty about its role. St Augustine's Kilburn though stands as a magnificent monument to Victorian certainty.

BIBLIOGRAPHY

Allen, F. J. *The Great Church Towers of England*, 1932

Anderson, M. D. *History and Imagery in British Churches*, 1969

Andrews, F. B. *The Medieval Builder and his Methods*, 1925

Barley, M. W., and Hanson R. P. (eds).
   Christianity in Britain 300-700 1968

Blatch, Mervyn. *A Guide to London's Churches*, 1978

Blue Guides. *Churches and Chapels: Northern England*
   edited by Stephen Humphrey, 1991

Blue Guides. *Churches and Chapels: Southern England*, edited by
   Stephen Humphrey, 1991

Braun, Hugh. *Parish Churches:*
   Their Architectural Development in England, 1970

Clark, Basil F and Betjeman John. *English Churches*, 1964

Clark, B. F. L. *Church builders of the Nineteenth Century*, 1938

Deansley, M. A. *A History of the Medieval Church 590-1500*, 1976

Eastlake, C. L. *A History of the Gothic Revival*, 1872

Hutton, Graham, and Cook, Olive. *English Parish Churches*, 1976

Gough, Richard. *The History of Myddle* edited by David Hay, 1981

Harvey, J. H. *The Medieval Architect*, 1972

Pevsner, Nikolaus and others. *The Buildings of England*, various dates

Josselin, Ralph. *Diary*, 1908

Kilvert, Francis. *Diary* edited by William Plomer, 1977

Knoop, D. and Jones G. P. *The Medieval Mason*, 1967

Platt, Colin, *The Parish Churches of Medieval England*, 1981

Prior, E. S. *A History of Gothic Art in England*, 1900

White, Gilbert. *The Natural History of Selborne*, 1841

Woodforde, James, *Diary of a Country Parson*, edited by John Beresford, 1953

INDEX

Churches are located under place names.
Numbers in *italics* refer to illustrations